Crime, Punishment and Justice

Please return before the last
date
Conta

Volume 223

Series Editor

Lisa Firth

Independence

Educational Publishers

Cambridge

First published by Independence

The Studio, High Green

Great Shelford

Cambridge CB22 5EG

England

© Independence 2012

British Library Cataloguing in Publication Data
Crime, punishment and justice. -- (Issues ; v. 223)

1. Crime--Great Britain. 2. Crime prevention--Great

Britain. 3. Criminal justice, Administration of--Great

Britain.

I. Series II. Firth, Lisa.

364.9'41-dc23

ISBN-13: 978 1 86168 608 4

Printed in Great Britain
MWL Print Group Ltd

CONTENTS

Chapter 1 Crime Trends

Chapter 2 Crime Prevention

Chapter 3 Criminal Justice

OTHER TITLES IN THE ISSUES SERIES

For more on these titles, visit: www.independence.co.uk

A note on critical evaluation

Because the information reprinted here is from a number of different sources, readers should bear in mind the origin of the text and whether the source is likely to have a particular bias when presenting information (just as they would if undertaking their own research). It is hoped that, as you read about the many aspects of the issues explored in this book, you will critically evaluate the information presented. It is important that you decide whether you are being presented with facts or opinions. Does the writer give a biased or an unbiased report? If an opinion is being expressed, do you agree with the writer?

Crime, Punishment and Justice offers a useful starting point for those who need convenient access to information about the many issues involved. However, it is only a starting point. Following each article is a URL to the relevant organisation's website, which you may wish to visit for further information.

Crime on your street revealed

Street-level crime and local policing information tells the public what's happening on their streets.

People will now for the first time be able to see what crime and anti-social behaviour has happened on their streets, access details about their neighbourhood policing team and find out about regular beat meetings all at the touch of a button, the Home Secretary announced today.

Interactive maps which can be accessed on computers and mobile phones will open the door on crime and policing information, allowing people to view crimes including burglary, violence and anti-social behaviour in their areas by doing a simple postcode search.

This transparent new level of crime and local policing information will ensure people can tell forces what their concerns about crime and disorder are, find out information about crime in their area and hold police to account for how well they are dealing with the issues that matter locally.

Transparency agenda

It forms a key part of the Government's transparency agenda making crime and anti-social behaviour data available in an open format so that communities, local services and developers can use it to help people engage with the police in a meaningful way.

Home Secretary Theresa May said: 'We want people to be able to see what crime is happening on their street and to be able to tell their local police if they have concerns, and challenge them about how issues are being dealt with.

'From today, this new information will allow them to do just that. This is a major achievement, reconnecting the police and communities through the power of information.

'But this is just the start. We want to build on this by working with the police and communities to explore how we can go further and faster and drive forward even greater transparency across crime, policing and justice.'

Police minister statement

Minister for policing and criminal justice Nick Herbert said: 'I have been an advocate of street-level crime mapping since seeing it work in Los Angeles so I am excited to see this website launched today, particularly as I believe it goes further and is more comprehensive than any other scheme. Police.uk will make England and Wales world leaders in this field, with every citizen able to access details about crimes on their streets.

'Together with the introduction of directly elected Police and Crime Commissioners, we are giving people the information and power to hold their local forces to account and ensure that crime in their neighbourhood is driven down.'

ACPO statement

The Association of Chief Police Officers' lead on crime information Deputy Chief Constable Neil Rhodes said: 'This new community-focussed approach means the public can access street-level crime information simply by entering their street name or postcode into the website.

Heavens! Where is all that awful crime happening?

Just down the road!

HOME OFFICE

'Links to local neighbourhood policing teams will also be available and will help to build community involvement in policing.

'Making information available to the public will not only help to raise awareness of how the police service is working to reduce crime and disorder in communities, but will help reduce the fear of crime and in areas where crime is occurring, provide encouragement to the public to support the police with information and remain watchful when appropriate.

'The interest of victims are at the heart of this new approach and the Government is also working with the Information Commissioner to ensure that the identities of individuals are protected whilst giving people the information they need to challenge their police force and change their communities.'

Quote from Louise Casey

The Commissioner for Victims and Witnesses Louise Casey said: 'Publishing information about street-level crime and policing helps local people hold the police to account for what they are doing to tackle it.

'Greater transparency is vital if the public are to have the confidence to report crime and victims are to get the help and support they rightly deserve.'

The Information Commissioner Christopher Graham said: 'I welcome the drive to improve accountability through greater transparency. Crime mapping can be an effective means of letting people know what crimes are taking place in their local area although care needs to be taken as this can potentially have an impact on the privacy of individuals such as victims or witnesses.

'We are pleased to have had the opportunity to provide advice about the privacy implications and that our advice has been incorporated into many of the safeguards that have been put in place. It will be important that this initiative is reviewed to ensure that the privacy safeguards are effective in practice.'

Notes

1 The website can be accessed from: www.police.uk

2 The interactive map allows access to six categories of crime; these are: burglary, robbery, vehicle crime, violence, other crime and anti-social behaviour (a total of all of these combined is also included).

3 In May 2010, the Prime Minister set out the Government's plans to open up data and information to the public. This included the commitment to, from January 2011, publish detailed local crime data statistics every month, so the public can get proper information about crime in their neighbourhood and hold the police to account for their performance.

31 January 2011

⇨ The above information is reprinted with kind permission from the Home Office. Visit www.homeoffice.gov.uk for more information.

Crime 'affecting fewer people'

One in six people was the victim of a crime last year, official statistics show.

The latest crime and justice survey estimated 874,000 crimes were committed in 2010/11, including 220,000 violent crimes.

That means 17.8% of people were a victim of crime, down from 19.3% the previous year.

The proportion who were the victim of a violent crime also fell, from 3.6% in 2009/10 to 3%.

People in Scotland were less likely to be the victim of crime than those in England and Wales, where 21.5% of people were affected.

Justice Secretary Kenny MacAskill hailed the new figures, saying: 'Scotland is becoming safer. Violent crime is down, fewer Scots are likely to become victims of crime and the risk of crime is lower in Scotland than in England and Wales.

'Recorded crime in Scotland is at its lowest level in 35 years. Reoffending rates are at an 11-year low and the 1,000 additional police officers that this Government has put on the streets are protecting the public.'

However, 45% believed the crime rate in Scotland had increased and one in 20 adults were repeat victims of property crime such as vandalism or housebreaking, while 1% suffered more than one violent crime.

In 24% of all violent crimes last year, the offender was reported to have had a weapon, with a knife used in 11% of violent crimes.

Victims believed the offender to be under the influence of alcohol in 63% of all violent crimes and to have taken drugs in 34% of such offences.

1 November 2011

HOME OFFICE / PRESS ASSOCIATION

Crime in England and Wales 2009/10

An overview of the findings from the British Crime Survey and police recorded crime.

Edited by John Flatley, Chris Kershaw, Kevin Smith, Rupert Chaplin and Debbie Moon

Introduction

This overview draws out the main themes from the report and considers how the results relate to the broader picture for crime trends internationally. While this is not a systematic review of the literature it discusses possible hypotheses for the reasons behind crime trends to place the results in a better context.

There are two main sources of official statistics on crime: the police recorded series and the British Crime Survey (BCS). The BCS is a nationally representative sample survey (now based on more than 45,000 respondents) of the population resident in households in England and Wales. As a household-based survey, the BCS does not cover all offences or all population groups. While police recorded crime has a wider coverage of offences (including crimes such as drug offences that are often termed 'victimless') and covers the entire population, it does not include those crimes not reported to the police. Both sources have their strengths and weaknesses but together provide a more comprehensive picture than either on its own. However, there are some gaps in coverage which need to be borne in mind when interpreting the findings in this report.

Crime trends

For the offence types and population it covers, the BCS is a better measure of long-term trends because it is unaffected by changes in levels of public reporting or in police practice in recording crime. The chart opposite illustrates overall crime trends from the BCS and police recorded crime and shows overall declines in crime in recent years. However, the police figures are influenced by changes in levels of public reporting and also police recording practice.

There is a clear pattern from the BCS of crime reaching a peak in 1995 with a subsequent decline, with overall BCS crime down by 50 per cent since 1995. There were important changes in police recording practice in 1998 and 2002 which served to inflate the police figures and resulted in divergence from BCS trends. After the bedding-in of these changes, there has been more convergence in police recorded crime and BCS crime, with trends becoming more similar over the last three to five years.

While estimates for crime from the BCS go back to 1981, the Home Office have figures on crimes recorded by the police going back over more than 100 years.[1] However, one problem in interpreting police figures over the long term is our limited knowledge of how public reporting and police recording practices have changed. For example, over the 20th century police recorded crime figures increased more than 70-fold; this will not simply reflect possible changes in levels of offending but will be substantially affected by a range of factors including changes in public reporting, police recording and coverage of new offences as well as increases in population size.

The most striking new finding within this report is that both the 2009/10 BCS and police recorded crime are consistent in showing falls in overall crime compared with 2008/09. Overall BCS crime decreased by nine per cent (from 10.5 million crimes to 9.6 million crimes), and police recorded crime by eight per cent (from 4.7 million to 4.3 million crimes).

These results may be seen as surprising given there were expectations that crime, particularly property-related crime, could rise in a period of recession. However, neither source shows an increase in levels of property crime during this period (though the full effects will not show through with the BCS until next year[2]) and indeed there have been some notable falls. For example, both sources are consistent in showing marked falls in vehicle

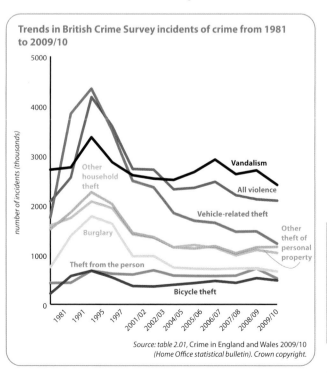

Trends in British Crime Survey incidents of crime from 1981 to 2009/10

Other household theft

Vandalism

All violence

Vehicle-related theft

Burglary

Other theft of personal property

Theft from the person

Bicycle theft

Source: table 2.01, Crime in England and Wales 2009/10 (Home Office statistical bulletin). Crown copyright.

HOME OFFICE

crime (BCS vehicle-related theft down 17 per cent and police recorded vehicle crime down by 16 per cent compared with the previous year). In addition, while the nine per cent fall in domestic burglary from the BCS was not statistically significant it is broadly in line with the six per cent reduction recorded by the police.

Provisional figures show that 7,995 firearm offences (representing 0.2 per cent of all offences) were recorded in England and Wales in 2009/10, a three per cent decrease from 2008/09

This is also the first time in recent years in which the UK Cards Association have reported a reduction in levels of credit card fraud with a two per cent reduction in the number of fraudulent transactions (down to 2.7 million in 2009 compared with the 2.8 million recorded in 2008) and a 16 per cent fall in UK fraud losses. A supplementary set of questions has been included in the BCS since 2005/06. In line with the UK Cards Association data, these have shown steady rises in the proportion of plastic card users who had been victims of fraud in the last 12 months (up from 3.4 per cent in 2005/06 to 6.4 per cent in 2008/09). However, the latest figures from the 2009/10 BCS are the first to show no increase. It is too early to say whether or not these findings represent a change in recent trends but they are notable nonetheless.

Trends in property crime

The results run counter to expectations based on previously published work on links between the economy and property crime trends (see for example Dhiri and Brand, 1999 and Field, 1990) which suggested that property crime would increase during a recession. The recent trends in property crime are part of a pattern of long-term decline with BCS acquisitive crime down by 55 per cent from its peak in 1995. There are a variety of reasons that may account for this and increasing security is an important one. The BCS shows increasing use of home security devices over this period and that these are associated with reduced risk of victimisation. For example, the 2009/10 BCS shows that households with 'less than basic'[3] home security measures were six times more likely to have been victims of burglary (5.8 per cent) than households with 'basic' security (0.9 per cent) and ten times more likely than households with 'enhanced' home security measures (0.6 per cent). Similarly, levels of vehicle security have also been enhanced in the period since 1995. Car manufacturers now fit immobilisers and other security features as standard to many of their models and such cars form a far greater share of the total stock than they did ten to 15 years ago.

Trends in violent crime

Violent crime contains a wide range of offences, from minor assaults such as pushing and shoving that result in no physical harm through to serious incidents of wounding and murder. In around a half of incidents identified as 'violent crime' by both BCS and police statistics, the violence involves no injury to the victim.

The BCS has adopted a consistent methodology over time and it is unaffected by changes in levels of reporting and recording of crime. Thus for the population groups and crime types it covers it is a better measure of long-term trends in violent crime than the police recorded crime series, which has been particularly affected by changes in the recording of violence against the person. However, there are some specific subcategories of violence not well covered in the main BCS crime count (such as homicide and sexual offences, see below).

Longer-term trends from the BCS show violent crime down by 50 per cent from its peak in 1995

There was not a statistically significant change in the number of violent crimes estimated by the 2009/10 BCS as compared with 2008/09 (the apparent one per cent decrease was not statistically significant). However, over recent years there has been an overall reduction in violent crime estimated by the BCS, consistent with trends in police recorded crime. Police-recorded violence against the person fell by four per cent between 2008/09 and 2009/10. Longer-term trends from the BCS show violent crime down by 50 per cent from its peak in 1995.

Homicide

The BCS does not measure homicide but it is well covered by the police figures as it is likely that relatively few homicides do not come to police attention. In 2009/10, the police recorded 615 homicides, down six per cent on the previous year (numbers are small for homicide but this figure would be judged to be statistically significantly below the final Homicide Index figure for 2007/08 of 753). The 2009/10 figures should be seen as provisional as the Homicide Index (see Smith et al., 2010) provides the definitive count for homicide, taking account of factors such as court decisions and deaths some time after an assault. However, these figures do suggest that in January 2011, when final figures are available, we may be reporting the lowest level of homicides since 1997/98 (the homicide levels in the 1980s and 1990s were not dissimilar to those that apply now, though they are higher than for much of the 1960s, when homicides were generally below 400 per year).

Results in Tavares and Thomas (2009) indicate that England and Wales has a homicide rate close to the average for EU countries at 1.4 per 100,000 population, with falls in homicide in most countries in the decade prior to 2007. The England and Wales figure remains well below the US homicide rate of 5.6 per 100,000 population despite figures both here and in the US having fallen in recent years (see discussion in Smith et al., 2010).

Sexual offences

The BCS does not include estimates of the number of sexual offences in its main crime count. However, it does provide estimates of the proportion of adults who have been a victim of such offences, which are obtained through a supplementary set of questions answered by self-completion outside the main interview. This shows that, according to the 2009/10 BCS, approximately two per cent of women aged 16 to 59 and less than one per cent of men (of the same age) had experienced a sexual assault (including attempts) in the previous 12 months. The majority of these are accounted for by less serious sexual assaults. There were no changes in the overall prevalence of sexual assaults between 2008/09 and 2009/10.

There were 54,509 sexual offences recorded by the police in 2009/10, a six per cent increase compared with 2008/09. This increase needs, however, to be interpreted with caution. The Association of Chief Police Officers (ACPO) has been taking steps to enhance the recording of serious sexual offences and this has culminated in inclusion of good practice guidance in the Home Office Counting Rules for crime from April 2010. While these were not formally in place in 2009/10, it may well be that figures for 2009/10 reflect initiatives undertaken by forces over the last year as they anticipated their introduction.

Guns and knives

There has been increasing public concern in recent years about gun and knife crime. While disturbing, the number of such crimes is relatively low and in a general population sample survey such as the BCS the number of victims is too small to produce reliable trend estimates. Additional data collections from the police provide better information on the number of such offences but cover only those that have come to the attention of the police.

Provisional figures show that 7,995 firearm offences (representing 0.2 per cent of all offences) were recorded in England and Wales in 2009/10, a three per cent decrease from 2008/09. This is in the context of firearm offences now being 22 per cent below the level in 2002/03, this being largely driven by reductions in imitation firearms rather than handguns and other firearms.

A special collection of knife crime data from the police was started in 2007/08 but comparable data are only available for the last two years. In 2009/10, for the selected offences[4], the police recorded 33,566 offences (representing around six per cent of the total offences in the selected categories and 0.8 per cent of all offences) where a knife or sharp instrument was involved, a fall of seven per cent from the previous year.

There are two additional sources of knife crime data presented in this bulletin: one covering the number of admissions to NHS hospitals in England involving wounds suffered as the result of assault with a sharp object and the other an annual survey covering a sample of emergency departments and walk-in centres in England and Wales. Although these figures can be affected by changes in NHS practice and recording, as well as the propensity of the public to seek treatment, they are not likely to be affected by police enforcement activity (or by public reporting to the police, or police recording practices).

The provisional 'Hospital Episode Statistics' for admissions show that in the 12 months from March 2009 to February 2010 there were 4,708 admissions for assault by a sharp object in England, four per cent less than the same period the previous year. This is in line with decreases seen in police recorded crime and the BCS, though hospital admissions will only involve the more serious incidents covered by these sources.

The latest survey in 2009 of emergency departments showed little change in violence-related attendances in 2009 compared with 2008 (there was an overall decrease of less than one per cent). Longer-term trends from this study have tended to reflect BCS trends in violence since 2002 when the emergency department survey started.

Notes

1   See http://www.homeoffice.gov.uk/rds/pdfs07/recorded-crime-1898-2002.xls

2   Respondents to the 2009/10 BCS were asked about their experience of crime in the 12 months prior to interview and thus the crime reference period spans from April 2008 (three to six months before the recession started) through to March 2010.

3   'Basic' home security refers to households fitted with window locks and double locks or deadlocks to outside doors.

4   Attempted murder, GBH with intent, GBH without intent, robbery, threats to kill, ABH, sexual assault and rape.

July 2010

⇨ The above information is an extract from the Home Office document *Crime in England and Wales 2009/10*, and is reprinted with permission. Visit www.homeoffice.gov.uk for more information.

HOME OFFICE

Troublesome youth groups, gangs and knife-carrying in Scotland

Information from the Scottish Centre for Crime and Justice Research.

SCOTTISH CENTRE FOR CRIME AND JUSTICE RESEARCH

Young people's views and experiences

Whilst some young people referred to the groups they were involved with as 'gangs', in general they resisted the gang label, preferring to talk about the people they hung about with in terms of an 'area', a 'team' or a 'group'. The groups were mostly small, with relatively narrow age ranges, though at weekends these groups might consist of as many as 30 to 60 young people.

The vast majority of the groups were mixed-gender, but predominantly male. Both male and female respondents reported that young men, in general, were more heavily involved in offending and violence than young women. Young women, in contrast, were perceived primarily as group associates. The groups can best be characterised as fluid and informal friendship networks that met regularly, but not in any formal capacity. Group membership and, for some, violent group behaviour were regarded as a normal part of growing up in particular families and neighbourhoods. Young people articulated an interweaving of individual, friendship and group identities, which in the West of Scotland were further underwritten by territoriality. The significance of territoriality was not nearly so strong in the East of Scotland.

The generic features ascribed to these groups by the young people themselves hold a resonance with the Eurogang network definition of a gang, this being: 'a street gang (or troublesome youth group corresponding to a street gang elsewhere) is any durable, street-oriented youth group whose identity includes involvement in illegal activity' (Weerman et al., 2009). Hereafter, we employ the term 'gang', using it as an umbrella term to encompass troublesome youth groups as well as groups engaged in more problematic behaviour inclusive of collective violence.

Young people reported a sense of belonging associated with gang membership, the interlocking of friendship and gang identities taking place at an early age, that membership was sought for self-protection and entailed backing-up your friends, and that fighting was seen as a way of developing a reputation and gaining respect. Essentially, gangs are not organised, but remain groups of adolescents looking for something to do, belonging, status and identity. Many aspects of their lifestyle are conventional and reflect those of other young people who do not associate with gangs.

Members reported participating in a range of anti-social and criminal behaviours including property damage, theft and public disorder offences, as well as violence. Drinking alcohol was a commonly identified pastime and recognised precipitator of violence. Drugs were readily available to young people but not everyone reported taking them. Very serious offending (including violent offending) was the preserve of a few 'core' gang members and did not necessarily take place within the frame of the gang.

Territorial fighting was the most common type of violence reported, particularly in the West of Scotland. Long-standing traditions and historical arguments were often mentioned as precursors to violence with a rival gang. In the East of Scotland, there was not the same degree of focus on the past battles or feuds. In addition, fights in the west were often orchestrated and planned, whereas violence in the east was more often described as opportunistic. Most fights were not serious and instead involved a great deal of bluster, posturing and stand-off. However, young people also reported occasions in which gang fights had led to serious injuries.

There was a certain degree of sex difference, with young women tending to be very much on the periphery of violent encounters and no expectation that they would participate. Both males and females appeared to operate according to an unspoken set of rules of engagement, which defined who fought with whom. For some young people, fighting provided a certain degree of excitement and thrill which they thrived on.

Attitudes towards weapon carrying and use varied enormously, with no clear trend or pattern being evident. Many carried weapons, but many others were opposed to the idea. Young people reported using a wide variety of weapons. Those that carried knives did so for a variety of reasons, as a means of self-protection (with no intention of use), as a weapon (with the intention of use) and to promote their reputation (use and non-use).

Most were aware of the physical and social risks of knife-carrying and/or use. Many (carriers and users) had been victims of knife attacks and were aware of risk of imprisonment (associated with being caught using a knife in a fight) and the longer-term risks to their social and economic wellbeing. This led some to desist from knife-carrying. Others chose to use alternate weapons. However, recognition of the risks appeared to hold a limited impact upon some from carrying or using knives.

Whilst many of those young people interviewed had not (yet) considered withdrawal, those that had were aware of there being significant barriers to exit. The intertwining of individual and gang identities acts as a significant inhibitor of withdrawal; to break from the gang requires a break from some of the key relationships in a gang member's life. However, most were able to articulate a range of negative outcomes associated with gang membership. These negative outcomes centred on restricted physical mobility for fear of assault by a rival gang. As those gang territories based on residential neighbourhoods are characterised as lacking recreational, social and economic resources, restricted mobility essentially restricts the opportunities open to a young person.

Those interviewees who claimed to have withdrawn from gang membership reported significant lifestyle changes. Some had simply grown out of gang fighting; it no longer held the excitement that attracted them in the first instance. Others were increasingly aware of the negative consequences. Crucially, a seemingly successful exit strategy rested in the establishment of new social and economic experiences and relationships.

Recommendations

There is a clear need to improve official data sources on youth crime, inclusive of youth gang activity and knife (weapon) carrying. Developing national standards and collating data on the qualities of gang members and knife-carriers will enable a more nuanced probing of the aetiologies of these behaviours to be achieved. This task is of fundamental importance for the design and delivery of effective intervention strategies.

The evidence collated in this study demands the development of area and group (age and nature of offending/anti-social behaviour) sensitive intervention strategies. Interventions with some youth gang members will be more appropriately framed according to their individual rather than group offending behaviour. Policy initiatives targeted at 'core' gang members may have a much wider impact on reducing youth disorder in terms of dispersing the gang through removing its central focus.

A core finding of this report is that gang members (inclusive of those who carry/use knives and other weapons) are drawn from areas of multiple deprivations. Strategies involving socio-economic improvement and increased opportunities for young people might be particularly beneficial. This suggests the need to integrate socio-economic strategies with gang intervention strategies.

Youth gang members (because of the nature and location of their behaviours) are likely to be highly visible as problematic individuals. Moreover, many of those known to the police and the children's hearing system

are at high risk of being in a gang. Therefore, there are a number of channels through which intervention strategies could be directed, including youth street work and the police, schools and social workers.

Criminal Justice strategies (policing and punishment) appear to influence the decision-making of some, but not all, gang members and knife-carriers. For example, stop and search strategies led some to no longer carry a knife though others reported carrying alternate weapons. Older gang members/weapon carriers are more sensitive to these strategies. The ease with which young people reported gaining access to knives and their ability to substitute a knife for another weapon suggests that knife amnesties will have a limited impact on violent behaviours using weapons.

Young people's awareness of the negative consequences of youth gang membership and knife-carrying implies that standalone and one-off awareness-raising (educational) strategies will have a limited impact in changing behaviours. Longer-term and early interventions, such as family and neighbourhood (anti-territorial) based intervention projects, which recognise the context of communities with long gang traditions, and aim to make available resources and services aimed at helping and supporting very vulnerable young people, may hold the potential to support long-term change.

⇨ The above information is an extract from the Scottish Centre for Crime and Justice Research's report *Troublesome Youth Groups, Gangs and Knife-carrying in Scotland*, and is reprinted with permission. Visit www.scotland.gov.uk for more information.

© Crown copyright 2010

SCOTTISH CENTRE FOR CRIME AND JUSTICE RESEARCH

Riots and rationality

Information from the Economic and Social Research Council.

The rioting and looting in London and other cities has led to shocked reactions from residents and victims, while the Prime Minister has vowed to 'restore order to Britain's streets'.

'Political reaction denouncing the London disorders as "wanton criminality" or "copycat rioting" have an understandable but distressingly familiar ring. Those involved in the disorders will undoubtedly have a variety of differing motives for engaging in such action,' says Professor David P. Waddington at Sheffield Hallam University.

'However, we can be virtually sure that the "flashpoint" or triggering incident which ignited the Tottenham disturbance and subsequent disorders will have crystallised widespread and enduring grievances concerning relations with the police and other sources of social disaffection.'

Professor Waddington has researched policing of public order and riot behaviour over several years.

In the ESRC-funded research project, *A Comparative Analysis of Recent French and British Riots*, he led a series of workshops looking at the 2005 and 2007 riots in the French banlieues and the 2001 riots in West Yorkshire and East Lancashire. After the 2001 riots, there were many suggestions of possible causes for the unrest – including ethnic segregation, lack of cultural integration, police misconduct and youth alienation.

Nineteenth-century French academics suggested that the 'group mind' of a rioting mob could explain acts of collective violence, emphasising the inherent suggestibility, amorality, and destructiveness of crowds.

In the *Sociology Compass* article 'The Madness of the Mob? Explaining the "Irrationality" and Destructiveness of Crowd Violence', Professor Waddington rejects this theory in favour of an analysis which demonstrates how even the most destructive acts of collective violence are typically underpinned by a restraining rationality.

Rioting is often seen as simply irrational. People have reacted to the London riots as being 'senseless', 'mindless violence' and 'without any reason or logic to it'.

'There is concrete academic evidence to show that institutions such as the police (not all of them but certainly junior to middle ranks) tend to think of rioting as irrational behaviour,' Professor Waddington points out in *The Browser*.

'There is this view that when people are in crowds, they are suddenly enveloped by the red mist. This kind of perspective is actually very unhelpful, not least to the police themselves.'

9 August 2011

⇨ The above information is reprinted with kind permission from the Economic and Social Research Council. Visit www.esrc.ac.uk for more information.

© Economic and Social Research Council

Young must be consulted on violence causes

Information from CYPNow.

By Janaki Mahadevan

Young people from areas affected by violence and looting have spoken out to condemn the riots and have called for more attention to be placed on young voices, as the causes of the outbreaks begin to be examined.

All 20 members of Enfield's youth parliament spoke of their shock at the destruction of parts of their community.

In a statement, the young people said: 'We are shocked and appalled by the destruction that has been caused by a small group of troublemakers, who are entirely unrepresentative of a majority of young people in Enfield.

'This behaviour is utterly unacceptable and only damages the perception of Enfield, our communities and young people as a whole. We hope that the violence comes to an end immediately and that we can take steps to ensure that this is not repeated again.'

Young reporters at youth magazine *Live*, which is based in Brixton, have been talking to young people around London to find out their thoughts on the riots.

Celeste Houlker, editor of *Live* magazine, said: 'The majority of young people are saying that they can't believe this has happened and they shouldn't have been looting and it is a terrible thing.

'It puts young people back a couple of years in terms of how we have been seen through the media.'

Referring to the current media coverage of the riots, Houlkter said she was concerned at how few young people are being asked to comment.

'I feel the media are not talking to young people enough,' she said. 'They should be trying to talk to young people who did the rioting as well to find out their reasons for doing it, to get to the cause of why it happened.'

A range of reasons have been cited by young people as to why a minority of their peers became involved in the events of the past few days.

'Some young people think it was because the opportunity was there and they went for it, some are saying they did it out of frustration because of all the cuts that have happened and because youth centres have gone,' Houlkter said. 'People our age are in a difficult position right now because we don't know how our future is going to turn out. Are we going to be home owners, will we all be in debt, what is our lifestyle going to be like, are we going to struggle or be independent?'

She added that while parents of children under the age of 16 should be held responsible for where their children were during the riots, those with teenagers had a more difficult job.

'Once you hit the age of 16 and you have made up your mind that no one is going to control you. It is very difficult to take control of a teenager and tell them what to do,' she added.

11 August 2011

⇨ Information from Children & Young People Now. Visit www.cypnow.co.uk for more.

Over 500 young people tell the Jack Petchey Foundation what they think about the rioting

Over 500 young people tell our 99% campaign partner, Jack Petchey Foundation, what they think about the rioting.

⇨ 50% think the cause of the riots was mindless violence: the rest say boredom (13.5%), lack of provision/interest in young (13.2%), lack of morals (10.6%), gap between rich and poor (6.6%) and youth unemployment (6%).

⇨ 5% were asked to get involved but less than 0.5% were actually involved.

⇨ 95% definitely would not take part if asked to, 2% would consider.

⇨ 63% got their information from TV/radio, not social networking (14%).

⇨ 45% feel the coverage of young people was unfair.

⇨ 86% think parents should take more responsibility for their children's crimes.

Half of the young people think that the main reason for the recent rioting across the country was simply 'mindless vandalism', as indicated by a snapshot survey of over 500 young people undertaken by the Jack Petchey Foundation. Others cited boredom (13.5%), lack of provision and government interest in young people (13.2%), lack of morals (10.6%), the gap between rich and poor (6.6%) and youth unemployment (6%).

Of the 517 respondents, 80% completely condemned the violence outright and 95% said they would not take part if asked to do so.

A number of young respondents pointed to the lack of morality in society generally, summed up by this young man: 'It's bad examples set by parents and the ruling elites. MPs' expenses, bankers' greed, bailout and continued bonuses, Murdochgate and cosy deals with media, police and government...'

The Jack Petchey Foundation believes it is particularly important to seek the views of young people as our society seeks to understand the causes. Many are angry that 'young people' have been blamed. Almost half (45%) felt the coverage of young people was unfair. One commented: 'The media are only interested in showing and talking about negativity against the youth.' Another said: 'I saw a headline which said "teenagers rob local shop". It's stupid because you wouldn't say "adults rob local shop"! It was not just youth who were involved in rioting and looting, but parents and adults as well. Unfortunately 95% of news reports failed to label the other age groups involved.'

It is really important young people are not scapegoated and blamed for these riots. 99% of young people are not involved in serious youth violence (London Serious Youth Violence Board) and if we focus on the 1% who are, we risk creating a negative cycle. As one young person said: 'If young people feel like they are treated as scum so they will act as scum.' Despite current debates about the role social networking played in inciting copycat behaviour, almost two-thirds of young people (63%) told us that TV/radio was the main source of information, with only 14% using Facebook and instant messaging as their provider of information.

There needs to be a focus on responsible reporting of such violence. It does not seem helpful that the same rolling images were being shown (as if live) on news programmes at least 24 hours after the events had actually taken place. Interestingly, of the young people surveyed, 86% thought that parents should take more responsibility for their children's crimes.

One of the outcomes of this situation has to be a long hard look at how society promotes parental support and creates opportunities for parents to engage and be proud of their youngsters. Our 2011 *Listen Up* report showed that over 66% of young people said that the most inspirational person in their life was a family member as opposed to celebrities, friends, etc.

Where there is a lack of parental support (for whatever reason), the Jack Petchey Foundation believes we have to create opportunities for alternative parent figures to engage with young people. Thousands of grassroots organisations work for the good of young people year on year and we know the difference this makes to many youngsters who might otherwise be 'lost'. The Jack Petchey Foundation plans to invest a further £300,000 this year in our Achievement Award programme (making a total of £2.8 million per annum) to inspire, support and affirm young people through these grassroots youth organisations who provide a sense of community, moral support and education for our youngsters.

Clearly there can be absolutely no justification for the violence that has occurred. Unlike previous riots in the UK, it seems that there is not one clear-cut cause and the underlying reasons are complex.

We call on government, policy-makers and community leaders not to make knee-jerk solutions to the situation but to engage with the communities directly affected, to engage with young people and to ensure that they feel their voice is heard, as we build our society for the future.

* Of the 5% (ten) who said they would get involved if asked – five said they would protest non-violently, not riot; three felt it would be exciting; one wanted to overthrow the Government, and one was scared what would happen to his family if he didn't.
13 August 2011

⇨ Information reprinted with permission from the Jack Petchey Foundation: www.jackpetcheyfoundation.org.uk

© Jack Petchey Foundation

Are criminals programmed to offend?

Information from the Criminologist blog.

The nature v nurture debate has been a hot topic in criminology for countless years. Are some people born with a criminal nature or do factors in their upbringing and environment shape them into criminals?

If the former is true, then could there be a way of identifying the criminals of the future while they are still young children?

And can they truly be held responsible for their crimes if they are biologically programmed to be anti-social?

At the annual meeting of the American Association for the Advancement of Science earlier this year, two leading criminologists laid out the evidence which they believe points to some biological factors being involved in criminal behaviour.

Professor Adrian Raine, of the University of Pennsylvania, told the meeting that differences between men's and women's brains might explain why males commit far more crime than females.

A part of the brain which controls emotion – the orbital frontal cortex – is much bigger in women's brains than in those of men, he explained. And no matter what their sex, people with proportionately smaller orbital frontal cortexes appeared to be more anti-social than those with normal-sized ones.

Also involved in emotion is the amygdala, which lies in the limbic portion of the brain, Professor Raine said, adding that a neural abnormality had been identified which was linked to anti-social behaviour. This abnormality occurred in the first six months of life.

'The seeds of sin are sown quite early on in life,' he commented. 'Individuals with this neural abnormality are more psychopathic, they are more anti-social, they commit more crimes than individuals who lack this limbic abnormality.'

He told the meeting about a research study which followed 1,800 people from age three to 23 and which found that, indeed, individuals with poor amygdala function in early life were more likely to become criminal offenders later on.

The meeting was also addressed by Professor Nathalie Fontaine, of Indiana University, whose researchers studied more than 9,000 twins, following their progress from age four to age 12. It found that genetic factors were involved in some conduct problems, particularly in the case of boys.

Both academics stressed that their findings are, as yet, too inexact to be safely used in predicting whether or not an individual will become an offender or what might be done to stop them.

But Professor Raine raised a fundamental question.

'If the psychopath has an amygdala which is shrunken by 18 per cent, which is functioning more poorly when they are making moral decisions, then how just is it for us to punish psychopaths as harshly as we do in the criminal justice system?' he asked.
27 May 2011

⇨ The above information is reprinted with kind permission from Criminologist. Visit http://criminology.blog.co.uk for more information.

© Criminologist

Chapter 2

CRIME PREVENTION

Reporting a crime

If you've been the victim of a crime or think you have witnessed one, you should report it to the police straight away. Your information could be used to prevent other crimes and help keep other people safe. Find out about the different ways of reporting a crime.

Dialling 999

If you've been mugged, badly hurt or attacked in any way, or if you've just seen a serious crime being committed, then you should ring 999 as soon as possible.

Your call should be answered within ten seconds. A trained staff member will ask you to describe what has happened and where you are. They may ask if you need any other emergency services, such as an ambulance.

If you want to report a minor crime, such as a stolen mobile phone, you should go to your nearest police station to report it, or call your local police force

If the situation is an emergency, a police officer will come to the scene to talk to you. They'll ask you to explain what happened, and they can help you decide what to do next.

Reporting non-emergency crimes

If you want to report a minor crime, such as a stolen mobile phone, you should go to your nearest police station to report it, or call your local police force. You can now use the phone number 101 to report minor crimes to the police in some areas.

By not using 999 for minor crimes, you're making sure that people in genuine emergency situations can reach the police quickly.

Non-emergency crimes can include:

⇨ vandalism;

⇨ graffiti;

⇨ abandoned cars;

⇨ pickpocketing.

Giving a statement

Whether you reported an emergency or non-emergency, you will have to give a statement to the police. That means that you'll have to tell an officer what happened to you or what you saw.

They may ask you questions or ask you to repeat yourself, to make sure the statement is as accurate and as detailed as possible.

When you've finished giving a statement, the police will usually read it back to you to make sure that their written account matches yours.

If you agree, you'll sign the statement and get a crime reference number. If you want to contact the police about the same incident in the future, you'll need to keep that reference number in a safe place.

If you're a victim of theft, you'll need to use the reference number when you tell your insurance company.

How to report crime anonymously

If you want to report a crime, but you do not want to be identified to the police, call Crimestoppers.

Crimestoppers staff will record your information and pass it on to the police so that it can be used to solve the crime.

Your call will not be traced, and you won't have to testify in court or give a full statement, no matter how useful the information turns out to be.

You can call Crimestoppers at any time on: 0800 555 111.

⇨ The above information is reprinted with kind permission from Directgov. Visit their website at www.direct.gov.uk for more information on this and other related topics.

© Crown copyright

DIRECTGOV

Ending gang and youth violence

A *cross-government report – executive summary.*

Gangs and youth violence have been a blight on our communities for years. The disorder in August was not caused solely by gangs but the violence we saw on our streets revealed all too vividly the problems that sometimes lie below the surface and out of sight.

Over the years, successive Government interventions, initiatives and funds have failed to work. A concerted, long-term effort is now needed.

Since August, a group of senior ministers – led by the Home Secretary, working closely with the Secretary of State for Work and Pensions – has undertaken a thorough review of the problem of gang and youth violence. They have visited a range of projects working to stop youth violence; heard from international experts about what works in the United States and elsewhere; consulted with senior police officers and local authority officials; and talked to young people themselves. Several key messages have emerged:

First, the vast majority of young people are not involved in violence or gangs and want nothing to do with them.

Second, the small number of young people who are involved have a disproportionately large impact on the communities around them in some parts of the UK. It is clear that gang membership increases the risk of serious violence.

And third, this small minority of violent young people is not randomly distributed and does not appear out of the blue. Some areas suffer significantly greater levels of violence than others; some individual and family risk factors repeat themselves time and time again.

The police and other agencies need the support and powers to protect communities affected by gangs and to bring the violence under control. But gang and youth violence is not a problem that can be solved by enforcement alone. We need to change the life stories of young people who end up dead or wounded on our streets or are getting locked into a cycle of re-offending. Only by encouraging every agency to join up and share information, resources and accountability can these problems be solved.

> ## *The vast majority of young people are not involved in violence or gangs and want nothing to do with them*

The Government has already set in motion a number of far-reaching reforms to address the entrenched educational and social failures that can drive problems like gang and youth violence. Our welfare reforms will give young people better opportunities to access work and overcome barriers to employment. Our education reforms will drive up pupil performance and increase participation in further study and employment. The new Localism Bill will give local areas the power to take action and pool their resources through Community Budgets.

Our plans to turn around the lives of the most troubled families will also be crucial. A new Troubled Families Team in the Department for Communities and Local Government, headed by Louise Casey, will drive forward the Prime Minister's commitment to turn around the lives of 120,000 troubled families with reduced criminality and violence among key outcomes for this work.

Not every area will have a problem of gangs or serious youth violence, so our focus will be on the areas that do. We will offer them support to radically improve the way their mainstream services manage the young people most at risk from gangs or serious violence. At every

When a younger person is accused of breaking the law, to what extent, if at all, do you think each of the following should be taken into account by the courts?

Legend:
- To a great extent
- To some extent
- To no extent
- Don't know
- Not stated

Category	To a great extent	To some extent	To no extent
Their intellectual ability	12%	51%	31% (4)
Their age	24%	66%	9%
Their emotional and psychological maturity	24%	57%	17%
Their ability to live independently of family support	9%	52%	35% (3)
Whether they have caring responsibilities for children under 16	24%	49%	22% (4)
Whether they have caring responsibilities for an elderly or sick family member	24%	50%	22% (3)

% 0   20   40   60   80   100

Fieldwork: 13 January-7 February 2011. Source: Parliamentary Panel Survey – MPs, ComRes.

HM GOVERNMENT

stage of a young person's life story, the mainstream agencies with which they have most contact – from health visitors, to GPs, to teachers, to A&E departments, local youth workers and Jobcentre Plus staff – need to be involved in preventing future violence. That means simple risk-assessment tools; clear arrangements for sharing information about risk between agencies; agreed referral arrangements to make sure young people get the targeted support they need and case management arrangements which bring agencies together to share accountability for outcomes and track progress.

The small number of young people who are involved have a disproportionately large impact on the communities around them in some parts of the UK. It is clear that gang membership increases the risk of serious violence

This report sets out our detailed plans for making this happen. Providing support to local areas to tackle their gang or youth violence problem. We will:

⇨ establish an Ending Gang and Youth Violence Team working with a virtual network of over 100 expert advisers to provide practical advice and support to local areas with a gang or serious youth violence problem;

⇨ provide £10 million in Home Office funding in 2012/13 to support up to 30 local areas to improve the way mainstream services identify, assess and work with the young people most at risk of serious violence, with at least half of this funding going to the non-statutory sector;

⇨ invest at least £1.2 million of additional resource over the next three years to improve services for young people under 18 suffering sexual violence in our major urban areas – with a new focus on the girls and young women caught up in gang-related rape and abuse.

Preventing young people becoming involved in serious violence in the first place, with a new emphasis on early intervention and prevention. We will:

⇨ deliver our existing commitments on early intervention which research shows is the most cost-effective way of reducing violence in later life. We will double the capacity of Family Nurse Partnerships and recruit 4,200 more health visitors by 2015 and will invest over £18 million in specialist services to identify and support domestic violence victims and their children (who themselves are at particular risk of turning to violence in adulthood);

⇨ assess existing materials on youth violence being used in schools and ensure schools know how to access the most effective;

⇨ improve the education offered to excluded pupils to reduce their risk of involvement in gang violence and other crimes;

⇨ support parents worried about their children's behaviour by working with a range of family service providers to develop new advice on gangs.

Pathways out of violence and the gang culture for young people wanting to make a break with the past. We will:

⇨ continue to promote intensive family intervention work with the most troubled families, including gang members, with a specific commitment to roll out Multi-Systemic Therapy for young people with behavioural problems and their families to 25 sites by 2014;

⇨ set up a second wave of Youth Justice Liaison and Diversion schemes for young offenders at the point of arrest, which identify and target mental health and substance misuse problems. These will be targeted at areas where there is a known and significant gang or youth crime problem;

⇨ work, through the Ending Gang and Youth Violence Team, with hospital Accident and Emergency Departments and children's social care to promote better local application of guidance around young people who may be affected by gang activity presenting at A&E;

⇨ explore the potential for placing youth workers in A&E departments to pick up and refer young people at risk of serious violence;

⇨ support areas, through the Ending Gang and Youth Violence Team, to roll out schemes to re-house former gang members wanting to exit the gang lifestyle;

⇨ explore ways to improve education provision for young people in the secure estate and for those released from custody;

⇨ implement new offending behaviour programmes for violent adult offenders in prison and under community supervision, including new modules on gang violence.

Punishment and enforcement to suppress the violence of those refusing to exit violent lifestyles. We will:

⇨ extend police powers to take out gang injunctions to cover teenagers aged 14 to 17;

⇨ implement mandatory custodial sentences for people using a knife to threaten or endanger others – including for offenders aged 16 and 17;

⇨ introduce mandatory life sentences for adult offenders convicted of a second very serious violent or sexual crime;

extend the work that the UK Border Agency undertakes with the police using immigration powers to deport dangerous gang members who are not UK citizens, drawing on the success of Operation Bite in London;

consult on whether the police need additional curfew powers and on the need for a new offence of possession of illegal firearms with intent to supply, and on the appropriate penalty level for illegal firearm importation.

> *Nationally, we are clear that our approach will stand or fall on whether it reduces the number of young people killed or seriously wounded – this will be our ultimate goal*

Partnership working to join up the way local areas respond to gang and other youth violence. We will:

issue clear and simple guidelines on data sharing that clarify once and for all the position on what information can be shared between agencies about high-risk individuals on a risk aware, not risk averse, basis;

promote the roll-out of Multi-Agency Safeguarding Hubs (MASH), which co-locate police and other public protection agencies, to cut bureaucracy and make it easier to share information and agree actions;

deliver on our commitment that all hospital A&E departments share anonymised data on knife and gang assaults with the police and other agencies and pilot the feasibility of including A&E data on local crime maps;

encourage the use of local multi-agency reviews after every gang-related homicide to ensure every area learns the lessons of the most tragic cases.

This report marks the beginning of a new commitment to work across government to tackle the scourge of gang culture and youth violence. An Inter-Ministerial Group, chaired by the Home Secretary and including the Ending Gang and Youth Violence team, will meet on a quarterly basis to review progress. We will also establish a forum of key external organisations to meet regularly with ministers and to hold the Government to account on delivery. We will ensure the views of young people themselves are heard too.

Nationally, we are clear that our approach will stand or fall on whether it reduces the number of young people killed or seriously wounded – this will be our ultimate goal. But crime figures only tell part of the story so we will work with local partners to agree other common-sense measures in high violence areas for individuals, families and communities. We will use these to help areas evaluate the impact of the measures outlined in this report. Our focus must now be on actions, not words.

November 2011

The above information is reprinted with kind permission from HM Government. Visit www.homeoffice.gov.uk for more information.

Schools at the sharp end of knife crime education

Young children in inner-city areas often have to face knife crime in their neighbourhood. Does it help them to tackle the issue head-on at school?

By Fran Abrams

In a classroom at St Ignatius Roman Catholic primary school in Tottenham, London, Alvin Carpio sits amid a circle of children, 24 pairs of eyes intently focused on him as he talks about his own childhood, a few miles away in east London.

'Whoever stole the most, or had the biggest knife, was the biggest man there. And you wanted to be that guy,' he says. 'We thought it was cool to steal – we really weren't making the right choices.'

Choices are the theme of the day for this class of nine- and ten-year-olds. Carpio, social outreach co-ordinator of the church next to the school, has been invited in to lead a drama workshop about good and bad decisions. The class have been acting out little scenarios: pick up that purse and take the money, or take it to the police? Bully the new kid at school, or make him a friend? But they know there's a darker theme underpinning the exercise. Carpio's visit is part of a class project on knife crime, and the aim is to make them think about decisions they may one day have to make about whether to carry a weapon.

St Ignatius is among a growing number of primary schools that have decided to tackle the issue head-on – often prompted by their pupils. According to the Citizenship Foundation, under whose auspices this class are running their project, knife crime is one of the top three issues named by this age group as their most pressing concerns, along with the environment and health. And although the charity hasn't yet assessed what proportion of schools taking up its 'Make a Difference Challenge' – under which children choose a topic to tackle in their local communities – are looking at knives or other violent crime, it says a very significant proportion have done so.

It is certainly a topic in which this class is interested, not to say fascinated. They start off shy – 'Why am I looking at three hands when I have 24 children in front of me?' exclaims the class teacher, Justa Fernandez. But within minutes there's a sea of waving hands and voices crying: 'Miss! Miss!' Everyone has an opinion. Some have suggestions about how to avoid getting involved: 'Sometimes you just have to say "no" to people,' Naysha, ten, suggests. Some want to share

their experiences: Evita, ten, tells a story about how her brother was mugged three times for his mobile phone. 'It was because he lived in N16,' she says. And some, particularly a few of the boys, just really want to share their knowledge on the subject. 'People just want you in their gangs, so they don't get in trouble – they stab people and run away,' says Jezreel, nine.

And that's hardly surprising: these children could hardly be unaware of the effect of knife crime in their local community. On the front of the church next door to the school hangs a huge banner, which reads: 'Isaiah 2:4: They will hammer their swords into ploughshares'. Underneath it is a knife amnesty bin into which people can place their weapons, dedicated to the memory of two young local men stabbed to death recently in separate incidents. One of them, a talented 17-year-old footballer named Godwin Lawson, who was killed last year, was a former pupil at St Ignatius, and some of Fernandez's class knew his siblings.

Nationally, knife crime is on the wane – there were 210 murders involving knives or other sharp instruments in 2009/10, compared with 270 two years earlier. Yet there's no denying it's a real issue for the children at St Ignatius. The children chose the project themselves after drawing up a list of things they'd like to change about their area. The final choice came down to a vote between knife crime and pollution – and crime won hands down.

Over the last three months, they've been building the subject into their normal lessons. Work on persuasive writing produced a list of slogans, now pasted boldly on to the white board: 'If you use a knife, you could delete a life', 'Drop that knife – don't waste my time'. A surgeon has been in to talk about her experiences of treating knife-crime victims, and the local police have also been invited.

The subject has clearly caught the children's imagination. Yet there's no suggestion any of these pupils have been tempted to get involved in gangs or knife crime themselves. So why are they so seized by the issue?

Fernandez says it's often on their minds: 'It's all around them; it's on the news. They'll often come in on a morning and say, "Did you see the news last night?"' she says. 'Godwin Lawson went to school with one of our girls' older brothers. She said in class that it made her sad when she heard his name mentioned.'

But while St Ignatius is in a high-crime, inner-city area, pupils from other districts are concerned, too. Marguerite Heath, director of Go Givers, the Citizenship Foundation's main programme for primary schools, says it's important to address their fears head-on.

'I think a lot of children do get quite concerned about this type of thing, particularly when they start to move on to secondary school,' she says. 'When they start to travel around on their own, rather than going by car. And I think on the whole we try to protect them too much, actually. A lot of this is to do with peer pressure – children get pressured into belonging to gangs, and this kind of programme gives them opportunities to rehearse the skills and practise the values they need to overcome that.'

'Whoever stole the most, or had the biggest knife, was the biggest man there. And you wanted to be that guy'

Leading campaigners on knife crime have argued that all children should learn how to make themselves safe – and should do so as early as possible. Earlier this year, Brooke Kinsella, the former *EastEnders* actress whose brother, Ben, was stabbed to death during a night out in north London in 2008, produced a report on the subject commissioned by the Home Office. It argued that all pupils should learn about knife crime during the last years of primary school, as the St Ignatius pupils have done this year.

But some sceptics say these efforts could prove counterproductive. Dennis Hayes, head of the Research Centre for Education and Career Development at the University of Derby, argues that there is a lack of solid evidence showing the effectiveness of such programmes.

'I think that unless they are thought through, initiatives with the best intentions can do a lot of damage,' he says. 'For most kids, knife crime isn't really an issue. Making them think about it is a bit like making people think about suicide. The message they get is that knife crime is a real problem, so perhaps they should carry a knife.'

Heath does not agree: 'I think if you don't address these issues that the children are thinking about, then misunderstanding grows and they can't get on top of it,' she says. 'The idea of the "Make a Difference Challenge" is that they are finding a way they can actually do something about it, so they feel empowered, and once you feel on top of something, it's no longer frightening.'

Some of the class have brought their own personal experiences in to share during the last two months. During our discussion, Olivia, ten, has been sitting with her hand up, but perhaps too shy to push herself forward. Eventually, Fernandez invites her to speak. 'Not long ago,' she says, 'someone stabbed someone near my house. And that made me think about knife crime. I felt that person's family must be really sad about what happened.'

The bilingual support assistant, Maria Miele, prompts her: 'Tell me what you told me when you came in that morning.'

'I thought maybe I would see them,' she says. 'And maybe they could do something to someone I knew.'

The headteacher, Con Bonner, says it's hardly surprising the children are frightened by such incidents when they happen so close to home: 'It's the environment where they're living,' he says. 'It's a topic that's discussed among young people generally. Literally in the streets they walk up and down, these events take place.'

31 May 2011

© Guardian News and Media Limited 2011

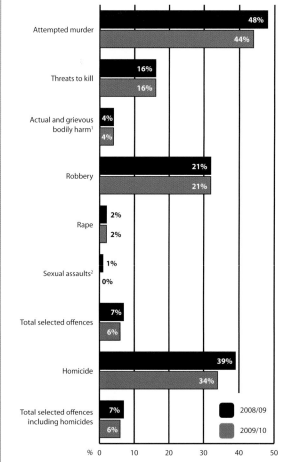

Proportions of selected violent and sexual offences recorded by the police involving knives or sharp instruments, by offence type: England and Wales (recorded crime).

- Attempted murder: 48% (2008/09), 44% (2009/10)
- Threats to kill: 16% (2008/09), 16% (2009/10)
- Actual and grievous bodily harm[1]: 4% (2008/09), 4% (2009/10)
- Robbery: 21% (2008/09), 21% (2009/10)
- Rape: 2% (2008/09), 2% (2009/10)
- Sexual assaults[2]: 1% (2008/09), 0% (2009/10)
- Total selected offences: 7% (2008/09), 6% (2009/10)
- Homicide: 39% (2008/09), 34% (2009/10)
- Total selected offences including homicides: 7% (2008/09), 6% (2009/10)

■ 2008/09
■ 2009/10

1. Includes wounding or carrying out an act endangering life.
2. Includes indecent assaults on a male/female, sexual assault on a male/female (all ages).

Source: table 3.13, Crime in England and Wales 2009/10 (Home Office statistical bulletin). Crown copyright.

THE GUARDIAN

Why ex-offenders should be given a role in cutting youth crime

Ex-prisoners have a lot to teach young people and will be listened to, says Stewart Dakers.

As the justice system struggles to address youth crime, there is one resource which could do more to retrieve and reform young people, to divert them from crime, and to restore a positive attitude in them than a dozen public enquiries and a battalion of QCs.

The people who know the streets, the youth on them, and what is in their heads, are people who have been there themselves, ex-prisoners. Yet they are never consulted.

I have worked with a number of ex-prisoners over the past ten years. I have witnessed their workshops, and seen the results. They are truly impressive. Agencies like UserVoice, Foundation4Life, and YouthempowermentCDS, are just some of the many initiatives undertaken by prisoners on release as they seek to put something back.

They are managed by ex-prisoners and employ other ex-prisoners. Selection is rigorous, training robust and supervision exemplary. These are remarkable men and women with an impressive product.

They deliver workshops across the country which aim to divert young people from crime by developing their sense of personal responsibility, by confronting them with the victims of crime, their families, and the community. They show them the consequences of crime for themselves and their life chances.

These are the only people who enjoy genuine credibility with 'the yoof'. It is not just that they have been there and got the T shirt. They know why the young people misbehave, because they did it themselves. They know how to encourage personal responsibility because they have acquired it the hard way. They know the consequences of crime, because they have experienced them big time, and still do. They know what triggers to squeeze, what sanctions to impose.

And they deliver. They have acquired a portfolio of skills in engaging with young people, which are beyond the imagination of the chuntering classes and, yes, most of the professionals. Time and again, I have watched a dozen young people, who would normally be off the wall within five minutes of attending a class, sit spellbound for two hours.

I have watched them at lunch break deep in conversation before returning for a further two hours still paying attention. It is a powerful, intense two-way process, with each, ex-cons and youth, exchanging painful, personal stuff, opening up, being vulnerable, sharing fears and hopes. In the pain and the tears, the young people rediscover a sense of purpose and of self. This is truly remedial work and it works.

Unfortunately, I have also witnessed the uphill struggle ex-offenders face. This is genuine resettlement, yet they continue to confront prejudice and incredulity. They are sidelined, ignored in the corridors. For all the extraordinary work they do, they remain engaged in a constant battle to make their voices heard, while political ears attend to the purveyors of judicial snake oil and the lucrative contracts are awarded to faithful amateurs.

The corridors are intellectually bankrupt on this issue but the cells have more than enough wisdom to confront it. We possess a rich seam of unused talent. Let's use it.

19 September 2011

THE GUARDIAN

Types of prison sentence

There are different types of prison sentences depending on how serious the crime committed is. Some are for a fixed length of time and others include a minimum amount of time before a person has any chance of release. Find out about the different types of sentences.

Why you could get a prison sentence

You could get a prison sentence if:

⇨ the crime you commit is so serious (for example, murder) that it's the only suitable punishment;

⇨ a court thinks the public must be protected from you.

If you have already spent time 'on remand'

If you have already spent time remanded in custody (in prison waiting for the trial), the time in custody is taken off your prison sentence.

If you're given more than one prison sentence

If you're convicted of committing more than one crime, you are usually given a sentence for each one. For example, if you commit a driving offence and the police also find illegal drugs on you, you will get a sentence for each offence.

Concurrent and consecutive sentences

Sentences for more than one offence can be served (carried out) concurrently or consecutively.

Concurrent sentences are served at the same time. Consecutive sentences are served one after the other – for example, a six-month sentence followed by a three-month sentence.

The judge (or magistrate) tells you what type of sentence you get and how it must be served.

Suspended prison sentences

If you get a 'suspended' prison sentence you don't go to prison immediately, but serve your sentence in the community. You have to meet certain conditions, which could include:

⇨ having to stay away from a certain place or person – for example, the victim of your crime;

⇨ doing unpaid work – called 'Community Payback'.

If you break any conditions, or commit another crime, you will go to prison to serve your sentence unless there are exceptional circumstances.

Prison sentences of a fixed length of time – 'determinate' sentences

A 'determinate' sentence is a prison sentence of a fixed length of time.

If your sentence is for 12 months or more

If your prison sentence is for 12 months or more, the first half of the sentence is spent in prison. The second half of your sentence is spent in the community 'on licence'.

Being on licence means you have to meet certain conditions. This could include having to stay away from the victim of your crime.

DIRECTGOV

If you break any conditions, or commit another crime, it's possible you could go back to prison to serve your sentence.

If you're on licence you are supervised (managed) by the Probation Service.

If your sentence is under 12 months

If your sentence is under 12 months, you are released automatically halfway through.

You are not supervised (managed) by the Probation Service but can still be sent back to prison – for example, if you commit another crime.

Prison sentences with no fixed length – 'indeterminate' sentences

A prison sentence that doesn't have a fixed length of time is called an 'indeterminate' sentence. This means you:

⇨ have no automatic right to be released at a set date;

⇨ have to spend a minimum amount of time in prison (called a 'tariff') before you can be considered for release.

The Parole Board is responsible for the release of offenders from prison.

Indeterminate sentences are given if a court thinks an offender is a danger to the public. They are usually given for violent or sexual offences.

Example of an indeterminate sentence

You commit a serious crime and are sentenced to a minimum of ten years in prison. After ten years, the Parole Board may decide:

⇨ it's safe to release you on licence – you're then supervised (managed) by the Probation Service;

⇨ it's not safe to release you – for example, because they think you are still a risk to the public.

Life sentences

If you get a life sentence, it lasts for the rest of your life – even if you're released from prison.

If you're found guilty of murder, a court must give you a life sentence. A court may also choose to give a life sentence for serious offences like:

⇨ rape;

⇨ armed robbery;

⇨ attempted murder.

You must spend a minimum amount of time in prison before being considered for release on licence.

If you don't meet the terms of your licence – for example, you commit another crime – you are likely to go back to prison.

Whole life term

In some very serious cases, a judge may give you a 'whole life term'. This means that there is no minimum term set by the judge, and you will never be considered for release.

⇨ The above information is reprinted with kind permission from Directgov. Visit www.direct.gov.uk for more information.

Changes to community sentences

Offenders will be made to do a full five-day week of hard work and jobseeking.

New plans for community sentences propose four days of hard manual labour, improving public areas by clearing up litter, cleaning graffiti and maintaining parks and other green spaces. The fifth day will be spent looking for full-time employment.

Previously, community payback programmes could be spread out over 12 months, with some offenders working for a minimum of just six hours per week.

The new, more intensive scheme will also be imposed on offenders within seven days of sentencing, instead of the two weeks it currently takes following a court appearance.

About 100,000 individuals are sentenced to community payback each year across England and Wales, with over 8.8 million hours of unpaid work completed last year.

24 August 2011

⇨ The above information is reprinted with kind permission from the Centre for Economic and Social Inclusion, based on information provided by the Ministry of Justice. Visit www.cesi.org.uk for more information.

New sentences to 'restore clarity and common sense'

Justice Secretary Ken Clarke has announced a new sentencing regime that will see more mandatory life sentences for a broader range of crimes. Brian Sims has the details.

Under the plans produced by Clarke and his team at the Ministry of Justice, more dangerous criminals will be given life sentences for crimes other than murder.

Mandatory custodial sentences will also be available for both adults and 16- to 17-year-olds convicted of aggravated knife and offensive weapon offences.

The announcement follows the Government's commitment to review the Imprisonment for Public Protection (IPP) sentence, which was criticised for being confusing and difficult to understand.

Justice Secretary Ken Clarke commented: 'The new regime will restore clarity, coherence and common sense to sentencing, rid us of the inconsistent and confusing IPP regime and give victims a clearer understanding of how long offenders will actually serve in prison.'

The new measures will be debated in the House of Commons next week and, if passed, will be added to the Legal Aid, Sentencing and Punishment of Offenders Bill (which is currently progressing through Parliament).

According to an official press statement, the new regime will include:

⇨ Mandatory life sentences – a 'two strikes' policy so that a mandatory life sentence will be given to anyone convicted of a second very serious sexual or violent crime (this will mean that mandatory life sentences can be given for crimes other than murder).

⇨ Extending the category of the most serious sexual and violent offences to include child sex offences, terrorism offences and 'causing or allowing the death of a child' so that the new provisions will apply to them.

⇨ The Extended Determinate Sentence (EDS) – all dangerous criminals convicted of serious sexual and violent crimes will be imprisoned for at least two-thirds of their sentence, marking an end to the regime which allowed the release of these offenders at the half-way point.

⇨ Offenders convicted of the most serious sexual and violent crimes in this category will not be released before the end of their sentence without Parole Board approval.

⇨ Extended licence period – criminals who complete an EDS must then serve extended licence periods where they will be closely monitored and returned to prison if necessary (the courts have the power to give up to an extra five years of licence for violent offenders and eight years for sexual offenders on top of their prison sentence).

⇨ Mandatory custodial sentence for aggravated knife possession – 16- and 17-year-olds – but not younger children convicted of using a knife or offensive weapon to threaten and endanger will face a mandatory four-month Detention and Training Order (DTO).

⇨ The Government has already announced proposals for a mandatory six-month sentence for adults convicted of the same offence.

Clarke continued: 'We intend to replace the widely criticised IPP system, which the public doesn't have confidence in, with a new regime of tough, determinate sentences. Under our plans we expect more dangerous offenders to receive life sentences. Those getting the new Extended Determinate Sentence will have to serve at least two-thirds of it behind bars before release. We're clear that there will be no automatic release before the end of the full sentence for the most serious cases.'

He went on to state: 'We have already announced that we are bringing in an automatic prison sentence for any adults who use a knife to threaten and endanger. Clearly any extension of this sentence to children requires very careful consideration. However, we need to send out a clear message about the seriousness of juvenile knife crime, so we are proposing to extend a suitable equivalent sentence to 16- to 17-year-olds, but not to younger children.'

Courts to see sensitive intelligence

New proposals allowing secret intelligence to be used in courts have also been announced by Ken Clarke.

The Justice and Security Green Paper will ensure that the sensitivity of evidence does not prevent cases being heard in the courts – enabling justice to be done without compromising national security.

The paper also sets out proposals to reform how the security and intelligence agencies are overseen and scrutinised.

INFO4SECURITY

Civil cases have previously collapsed because vital evidence could not be given in a public courtroom for fear of compromising national security and public safety.

The new proposals will mean changes to civil court procedures so that courts can take account of more material, with safeguards in place to protect national security.

The Green Paper also includes proposals to modernise the Intelligence and Security Committee (ISC) – granting it increased powers and independence.

All facts of a case must be considered

Clarke commented: 'For justice to be done and the rule of law to be upheld, courts should be able to consider all of the facts of the case. At the moment we're not always getting at the truth because some evidence is too sensitive to disclose in open court.'

The Justice Secretary added: 'The proposals in this Green Paper are based around the principles of rigorous, impartial and independent justice, fairness and proportionality. New measures will be balanced by enhanced safeguards and mechanisms to make sure that individuals' rights are protected, the process remains fair and that justice can at last be done.'

The Green Paper Consultation will remain open until 6 January 2012.

27 October 2011

⇨ The above information is reprinted with kind permission from info4security. Visit www.info4security. com for more information.

© *info4security*

FBI-style crime agency to lead fight against drug gangs

The Home Secretary is due to give more details of the new National Crime Agency, the Coalition's successor to Labour's heavily criticised SOCA unit.

A new FBI-style crimefighting agency will target drug gangs and paedophiles as well as helping to police Britain's borders, the Home Secretary has said.

Theresa May is expected to give more details of the National Crime Agency (NCA) in a Commons statement later.

The agency, due to be launched in 2013, will replace the Serious and Organised Crime Agency (SOCA).

It will also include a border police component and take in the work of the Child Exploitation and Protection Centre (CEOP), although CEOP will retain its own brand and budget.

Ms May said: 'We will bring together resources across a number of agencies which means we can deal with these things and have much more ability to deal with serious and organised crime.'

She said there would be no new money for the agency and the cost of setting it up would come from existing budgets.

The Home Secretary added: 'SOCA is not going to be disbanded. It will continue but as part of the new NCA, bringing together law enforcement across a number of types of crime at a national level that will enable us to really focus on organised crime.

'The drugs on the streets, these are being brought in by organised crime groups and these are the issues affecting neighbourhoods across the country.'

SOCA was described as 'Britain's FBI' when it was launched in 2006, but the agency was criticised for failing to fulfil its brief of bringing down Britain's 'Mr Bigs'.

The Home Affairs Select Committee described its performance as 'disappointing' in 2009 after it emerged that it was seizing £1 from gangs for every £15 in its budget.

CEOP's chief executive Jim Gamble resigned last year when it was announced the anti-paedophile unit would be merged into the NCA, saying the decision was not in the interests of children.

The unit said last month that it had helped arrest 1,644 suspected child abusers in the last five years, and dismantled 394 paedophile rings.

8 June 2011

⇨ The above information is reprinted with kind permission from Channel 4 News. Visit www.channel4. com for more information.

© *Channel 4 News*

INFO4SECURITY / CHANNEL 4 NEWS

Breaking the cycle

Clinks briefing on the Government's response to Breaking the Cycle and the Legal Aid, Sentencing and Punishment of Offenders Bill.

Introduction

The Government has published a written response to the *Breaking the Cycle* Green Paper consultation. This was accompanied by a Bill to alter the legislative framework for the reforms, *Legal Aid, Sentencing and Punishment of Offenders Bill*.[1] The Bill received its first reading in Parliament on 21 June 2011 and will next go for a second reading, at which point it may be debated in the House of Commons.

The Government response to the *Breaking the Cycle* consultation marks a retreat from some of the more radical suggestions outlined in the Green Paper earlier this year. Disappointingly, a statement in the foreword explicitly states 'we are not aiming to cut the prison population'. This has been perceived in many quarters as a u-turn on criminal justice policy and gives rise to concerns over where the missing £130 million will now be saved.

The Government response is a fairly short document that includes little detail about how Voluntary and Community Sector (VCS) organisations are to be financed and supported. We expect this to be expanded upon in *Competition Strategy for Offender Services*, to be published shortly.

This briefing notes the key provisions contained within the Government response and the Bill. Clinks will shortly be preparing a response to the Government paper and we invite our members to contribute their views and comments.

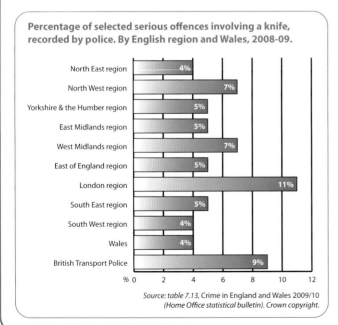

Percentage of selected serious offences involving a knife, recorded by police. By English region and Wales, 2008-09.

Region	%
North East region	4%
North West region	7%
Yorkshire & the Humber region	5%
East Midlands region	5%
West Midlands region	7%
East of England region	5%
London region	11%
South East region	5%
South West region	4%
Wales	4%
British Transport Police	9%

Source: table 7.13, Crime in England and Wales 2009/10 (Home Office statistical bulletin). Crown copyright.

Working prisons

⇨ Create a working week of up to 40 hours for prisoners.

⇨ Focus the daily regime around work.

⇨ Ensure prison work is sustainable and self-financing.

⇨ Focus education and training in prisons on equipping offenders to work, and link work activity to qualifications and employment opportunities on release.

The Bill allows for a portion of the prisoner's earnings, within prison and when working outside on licence, to be deducted to go towards victim support services. The proposal is for a 40% deduction after National Insurance and Tax.

The implementation strategy for work in prison will be published in the autumn. The Ministry of Justice is setting up a Business Advisory Group and also collaborating with the Department of Work and Pensions to link proposals with the Work Programme.

Community sentences

The Ministry of Justice (MoJ) aims to make community penalties more credible; focusing on 'punishment, control and reform' of offenders.

⇨ Courts will have the power to prohibit foreign travel and impose longer curfews.

⇨ Compliance panels will be established to ensure that young offenders comply with their sentences. This summer, in Norfolk and Suffolk, the MoJ are piloting a scheme under which offenders who persistently refuse to pay fines will have items seized, such as cars and TVs.

⇨ Increase use of financial penalties, both on their own and alongside other sentences.

⇨ Community Payback to be more intensive and demanding, with longer days and a working week.

Progression

The Government response states a number of priorities, aside from punishment, including getting offenders off drugs and alcohol, addressing offenders' mental health problems, helping offenders into employment and reducing the barriers to resettlement. In custody, this will mean moving to a system of recovery.

CLINKS

⇨ In five prisons, Drug Recovery Wings will be piloted; focused on providing continuity of treatment for short-term, drug-dependent prisoners between prison and the community.

⇨ The 'Virtual Campus' will be rolled out to broaden the range of employment and learning services available in custody.

⇨ In the community, opportunities for intensive drug and alcohol treatment-based accommodation will be considered. There are already eight local areas piloting payment by results approaches to drug and alcohol recovery.

⇨ For offenders with mental health problems, the MoJ is working with the Department of Health and the Home Office to pilot and roll out liaison services in police custody and at courts by 2014.

⇨ Separate consultation on offending linked to severe personality disorder will be published later this year.

⇨ Scheme led by Crisis to improve access to private rental sector for single homeless people.

⇨ Wider use of Bail and Support Service Schemes to reduce extent to which remand is used because offenders do not have stable accommodation.

⇨ MoJ to support a Ministerial Working Group on Homelessness.

Payment by results

⇨ A number of payment by results pilots have already begun in prisons and the community and there will be a competitive process this summer to commission further pilots.

⇨ Timetable for payment by results will be contained in the wider *Competition Strategy for Offender Services*.

Transparency

The MoJ aims to give victims and the public a better understanding of the Criminal Justice System (CJS) and opportunities to get involved.

⇨ More information to be published about sentencing, justice outcomes and local justice services.

⇨ Community priorities to inform the justice process.

⇨ Increased accessibility of information on volunteering opportunities.

⇨ Continue testing Neighbourhood Justice Panels to bring local volunteers and criminal justice professionals together.

A more central role for victims

⇨ Forthcoming victims' consultation.

⇨ Restorative justice interventions at every stage in the justice system.

⇨ MoJ to work with Home Office to develop a framework that supports local practitioners to develop effective restorative justice approaches.

Reforms to the justice system

⇨ Development of a national framework for out-of-court disposals to be published later this year.

⇨ Remand only to be used where necessary to protect the public where alleged offending is serious enough to warrant custody, including a risk of domestic violence.

⇨ New offence with mandatory minimum prison sentence of six months for adults for possession of a knife to threaten or endanger.

⇨ Review of serious sexual and violent offenders and IPPs, with view to replacing IPP regime with determinate sentencing framework.

　↳ Increased number of serious offenders would receive life sentences.

　↳ Serious sexual or violent offenders would spend at least two-thirds of their sentence in prison.

CLINKS

- Give courts greater discretion to use suspended sentences for up to two years, choose whether or not to impose community requirements, and have additional options of imposing fines for breach.

- Create a single set of rules for the operation of Home Detention Curfew.

- Allow greater professional discretion to decide when low-risk prisoners who have been recalled to prison may be released on licence.

Simplifying performance management

- More discretion for how probation services manage offenders.

- Performance of Probation Trusts and Prisons to be measured according to the outcomes of reducing reoffending, rather than by inputs and processes.

Youth justice

- Transfer functions of Youth Justice Board (YJB) to newly created Youth Justice Division in the MoJ (distinct from the arrangements in place for adults and led by the current Chief Executive of the YJB).

- All young people who are remanded will be recognised as 'looked after' by the local authority. All children under 18 to be treated the same, rather than treating 17-year-olds as adults.

- Local authorities to be financially responsible for all youth remands to secure accommodation to create an incentive to invest in alternative strategies.

Reducing number of foreign national prisoners

- Prisoner transfer arrangements so that EU nationals sentenced here serve their sentences in their country of origin come into force from December 2011.

- Deport foreign national prisoners on indeterminate sentences once they have served their minimum custodial term.

- Pilot use of cautions to divert from prosecution foreign nationals who do not have leave to stay in the UK and have committed certain crimes, on condition that they leave the UK.

Legal Aid, Sentencing and Punishment of Offenders Bill

Sentencing

- Imposes a duty on courts to consider Compensation Orders for certain types of offence.

- Increases the length of prison sentence that can be suspended, giving the court discretion not to impose community requirements as part of the sentence and enabling it to impose a fine for breach of a suspended sentence order.

- Extends the maximum curfew from 12 to 16 hours a day and from a maximum period six to 12 months.

- Makes amendments to the Mental Health, Drug Rehabilitation and Alcohol Treatment requirements.

- Creates a new power to prohibit foreign travel as part of an order.

- Amends Youth Referral Orders to provide more flexibility and discretion for their repeated use.

Bail

- Restrict the court's powers to remand unconvicted adults in custody where it is apparent that there is no real prospect that the defendant would receive a custodial sentence if convicted. A court would still be able to remand in custody for the defendant's own protection, or where there was a risk of further offending involving domestic violence.

- Children who are held on remand will have to be recognised as 'looked after' by local authorities.

- Imposes more rigorous requirements before under-18s can be remanded into youth detention accommodation.

Prisoners

- Gives the Secretary of State the power to make rules in respect of the employment and payment, including reductions in or deductions from such payments.

Knives and offensive weapons

- Creates new offences of threatening with an offensive weapon or an article with a blade or point, creating an immediate risk of serious physical harm. There will be a minimum sentence of six months' imprisonment for persons over 18 found guilty of this new offence.

Note

1   The full Bill and its progress through Parliament can be viewed at: http://services.parliament.uk/bills/2010-11/legalaidsentencingandpunishmentofoffenders.html

June 2011

- The above information is reprinted with kind permission from Clinks. Visit their website at www. clinks.org for more information on this and other related topics.

CLINKS

Prejudged: tagged for life

A research report into employer attitudes towards ex-offenders – executive summary.

Helping ex-offenders to find employment is key to helping people reintegrate into society. As a provider of services to offenders, we commissioned ReputationInc (a leading reputation management consultancy) to conduct a research study, and this report presents our findings. Following a review of previous research, we identified the main issues which affect the employment rate of ex-offenders. This helped to develop and inform our primary research, examining the views of employers when considering ex-offenders for vacancies. We also conducted a series of interviews with UK employers and an online survey of 300 UK employers. The key findings and recommendations to come from the research follow.

Exploring the relationship between employment and offending

The review of previous research on offenders and employment found that:

⇨ Over 17% of the UK population between the ages of 18 and 52 have a criminal conviction.

⇨ Reoffending has been estimated to cost the UK around £11 billion per year,[1] with each reoffending ex-prisoner potentially costing the criminal justice system alone an average of £65,000. Prolific offenders will cost even more.

⇨ Reoffending rates are greatly influenced by whether a person finds work or not. Employment is often quoted as the most important factor in helping to reduce reoffending rates.

⇨ There is a wide range of social and economic implications of the low employment rates of people with convictions, including housing, debt and finance, health and family relations – our report, however, concentrates on employer attitudes to ex-offenders. But this doesn't mean that we consider this the only problem to solve.

Employer perceptions of ex-offenders

Based on the analysis of previous research, we conducted an online poll to find out the attitudes and views of employers about ex-offenders.

⇨ We found conflicting views amongst employers. Although only 10% of employers told us they would not consider employing ex-offenders, only 18% said they have actually employed someone they know to have convictions.

⇨ Ex-offenders have a largely negative reputation amongst the employers who had no known experience of working with them. This is in stark contrast to the positive impressions of those employers who are open to recruiting ex-offenders.

⇨ When employers were asked what impact the disclosure of a conviction would have on their decision-making process, almost three quarters told us they would use this information to either reject the candidate outright (16%), or to discriminate in favour of an equally qualified candidate with no convictions.

⇨ Employers perceive ex-offenders as not having soft skills, such as honesty or reliability. These perceptions are challenged by the actual experience of employers taking on ex-offenders.

⇨ The type of offence committed is a significant factor in employer attitudes about recruiting ex-offenders. Driving and alcohol convictions are the only offences ignored by a significant majority of employers.

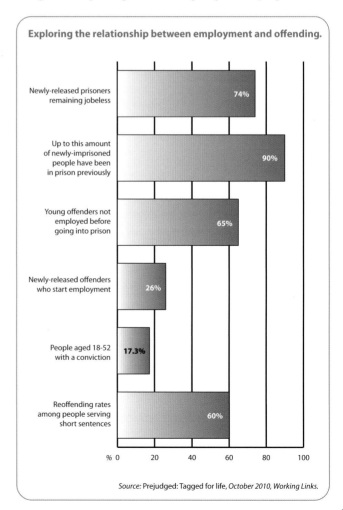

Exploring the relationship between employment and offending.

Newly-released prisoners remaining jobeless	74%
Up to this amount of newly-imprisoned people have been in prison previously	90%
Young offenders not employed before going into prison	65%
Newly-released offenders who start employment	26%
People aged 18-52 with a conviction	17.3%
Reoffending rates among people serving short sentences	60%

% 0   20   40   60   80   100

Source: Prejudged: Tagged for life, October 2010, Working Links.

The results of this research, together with our experience of working with both offenders and employers, have helped us to shape these key policy recommendations to the Government.

1. Implement the recommendations of the review of the Rehabilitation of Offenders Act (ROA)

In 2003, the then-Government accepted the recommendations of a review of the ROA. The ROA helps to define the responsibilities of ex-offenders. The review suggested changes that would further strengthen it, as well as considering the definition of the responsibilities of employers. We call upon the current Government to implement these recommendations.

2. Consultation on a new 'Offender Discrimination Act'

We recommend for there to be a consultation on a new Offender Discrimination Act to stimulate employers to consider hiring ex-offenders. This should identify clearer processes to support employers through information, advice and guidance, and investigate ways of protecting ex-offenders against discrimination. We see the key areas to be:

⇨ fewer jobs should require disclosure, and disclosure should be limited to more serious offences;

⇨ a more flexible application of disclosure rules. This would enable people within offender management services to play a role in reducing disclosure periods where they feel it is needed; and

⇨ protected positions. We recognise the need for some vacancies, especially around children and other vulnerable people, to require enhanced disclosures.

3. Financial incentives

Consider financial incentives to encourage employers to hire people with convictions, despite the perceived risk.

We have also made recommendations for offender services based on our employer research. These services and government must work together as an effective partnership in order to bring real benefits to people who are trying to move on from their past.

4. At the prison gate

Much greater support is needed for offenders while they are in prison to prepare them for release, and after release.

5. Greater communication and promotion of offender services

We need to increase awareness of the benefits of working with ex-offenders. Providing details about the business case, the real versus the perceived risk and case studies of success, will all help to improve demand for employing people with a conviction history.

6. Development of more support services for employers

There are calls for more expert advice and support, before and during employment. Providers of offender services have detailed knowledge in this area and are well placed to offer clear guidance about recruitment policies and issues related to recruiting and working with ex-offenders.

7. Greater support to ex-offenders in skills training, job-search and in-work support

We recognise that the skills and readiness for work of ex-offenders is a key factor for helping people into employment.

Note

1   National Offender Management Service, *Reducing re-offending through skills and employment: next steps*, p6 + Social Exclusion Unit Summary of *Reducing re-offending by ex-prisoners*, 2002, p1

October 2010

⇨ The above information is an extract from Working Link's report *Prejudged: Tagged for life*, and is reprinted with permission. Visit www.workinglinks.co.uk for more information.

© Working Links

WORKING LINKS

Restorative justice after the riots?

As a former young offender I know rehabilitation in prisons is lacking. But it was a letter from my victim that made me change.

By Paul Carter-Bowman

After the crimes, the punishment. Sentences handed down barely a fortnight after the mass riots across England have included prison terms of up to four years, where those on the receiving end will spend around two entire years in prison, with the latter part of their terms served on probation within the community. Of the 1,474 who have already appeared before the courts, over 1,000 have been remanded to custody, which, to you and I, means spending time in prison.

But what can we expect our prisons to achieve with these rioters?

In 1999, at the age of 16, I phoned the police and handed myself in for a violent offence I had committed the previous evening. I did this thinking that the punishment I would receive would be no more or less than what I deserved, and believed that it would serve a purpose beyond simplistic retribution. I was aware that I had overstepped the boundaries set down by society, that I had become a dangerous individual. I expected to be taught a lesson and, perhaps naively, that I would emerge from my punishment a reformed character.

However, from the moment I entered Reading young offenders institution, it was clear that the practice of prison did not include reform or rehabilitation. There was no interest from either the regime or the guards who kept us. The point of prison was simply to keep me there. This would, theoretically at least, make sense if I was to never be released. But after pleading guilty to grievous bodily harm, the sentence I received was four and a half years (I went on to serve three).

Indeed, of the thousands of young people aged 15 to 21 whom I shared prisons with, not a single one received a sentence that would keep them out of society for their anticipated natural lives. A couple committed suicide, one was murdered by his cell-mate, and several will still to this day be awaiting parole from a life sentence, but everyone else has since been released back into the community. Ministry of Justice data confirms that 75% of young people reoffend within a year of being released from prison, and no doubt many of the others just evade capture.

There are those who argue that the reason for the high rate of recidivism is due to prison being too soft and too comfortable – a place where prisoners can watch TV all day and play PlayStation. Yet research in Italy and the US suggests that far from reducing re-offending rates, harsher prison conditions may actually increase re-offending. And prisons in England and Wales are not exactly cushy. The final 18 months of my prison term was spent on a wing in Portland YOI where there was no in-cell sanitation and according to the most recent Prison inspectorate report in July 2009, it still had 'conditions [which] can only be described as squalid'.

The problem with our prison system is not that prisoners get to watch TV and play games, or that they get fed three (undelightful) meals each day. The problem is what they are not doing in prison. For the limited period of time that I was offered education, classes lasted only a few hours. The quality of teaching was poor, and the negligible expectation of the teachers was matched by the low ambition and efforts of the students – going by recent reports, things haven't changed.

I SENTENCE YOU TO HAVING YOUR CRIMINAL CAREER PUT ON HOLD

I did an anger management course (quite important for a violent offender), but this lasted just one hour per week. So what was I to do with the remaining 26,200 hours of my imprisonment? The vast majority of my time was spent rotting away in my cell, and the time spent out of my cell was more often than not punctuated by fear and intimidation.

Sadly, the criminal justice system in England and Wales does very little to foster communication between the offender and the offended

Around the time of my 18th birthday, I received a three-page letter from the victim of my offence. In this letter he explained the impact the offence had had upon him – how his family had been distraught, and how his emotional suffering had long outlasted his physical pain. I really don't know what I should have expected, but somewhere along the way I had neglected to consider my victim. Receiving this letter brought home every aspect of the offence that was the reason for my punishment. The most interesting point he made, was that he was in recovery, and wanted the same for me.

Of course, it didn't reform me instantly; it was no magic bullet. But it certainly brought me to my senses and stopped my further decline. Sadly, the criminal justice system in England and Wales does very little to foster communication between the offender and the offended, with restorative justice programmes being made available in less than 1% of cases.

However, one need not rely on the justice system for such contact to be made. To those who have been victims of the recent riots (or indeed any crime) where a perpetrator has been identified and sentenced, I would strongly encourage them to do as my victim did, and write a letter (for example, by using the prisoner location service), where they can convey their hurt and anger directly to the prisoner.

As society's ultimate rejection, prison is intrinsically destructive. But seeing as we plan on releasing all the recent rioters from prison at some point, it might not be such a bad idea to work towards increasing their empathy towards those they have hurt.

27 August 2011

Children 'not facing harsh riot sentences'

Information from Children & Young People Now.

By Neil Puffett

Children are not being sentenced more harshly for crimes associated with riots across cities in England earlier this month, the vice-chair of the Magistrates' Association has said.

Since people began appearing in court facing charges for public offences and theft in relation to the riots, there has been concern that children have been getting tougher sentences than they would have received for the same crimes in different circumstances.

John Fassenfelt, vice-chair of the Magistrates' Association, told CYP Now he believes this may be true for adults but believes minors are not being sentenced more robustly than usual.

'Our response to youngsters hasn't really changed,' he said. 'We are very cautious about remanding them in custody but mindful that they shouldn't commit further offences.

'Magistrates have been sentencing in line with the guidelines unless there are exceptional circumstances to do otherwise.

'I don't see any evidence of a tougher sentencing environment for children.'

Fassenfelt's view is not shared by Gareth Jones, vice-chair of the Association of Youth Offending Team Managers, who said he believes children are being given tougher sentences as a result of public and political demands.

He said an 11-year-old boy who was today given an 18-month youth rehabilitation order for stealing a bin during riots, would likely not have received such a sentence had it been an unrelated event.

The boy, from Romford in east London, was already subject to a referral order for an incident in July when he cut the seats of a bus with a knife and tried to set fire to the foam.

'It [the bin theft] was a relatively minor offence and you would expect the referral order to be extended,' Jones said.

31 August 2011

⇨ The above information is reprinted with kind permission from Children & Young People Now. Visit www.cypnow.co.uk for more information.

From playground to prison

The case for reviewing the age of criminal responsibility.

Background

⇨ The minimum age of criminal responsibility in England and Wales was set at ten in the 1963 Children and Young Person's Act. Previously the 1908 Children Act set it at seven.

⇨ In the 1998 Crime and Disorder Act, Labour abolished the principle of *doli incapax* whereby the prosecution had to prove that a child under 14 appearing in the criminal court knew and fully understood what he or she was doing was seriously wrong.

Statistics

There are essentially two ways of looking at the amount of crime committed by children aged ten and 11 in England and Wales:

⇨ The number of children given a youth justice disposal: custodial sentences, community sentences, pre-court reprimands and final warnings.

⇨ The number of proven offences that result in a disposal: a more accurate figure as one child can commit more than one offence, it gives the best current picture of the totality of known crime committed by the age group.

The number of ten- and 11-year-olds given youth justice disposals declined from 7,487 in 2005 to 5,671 in 2008, a fall of 24 per cent. What is most significant is that during a similar period, the number of offences committed by this group declined from 8,163 to 6,059, a fall of 26 per cent.

Convictions, sentences, reprimands and final warnings

There were 5,671 children aged ten and 11 in receipt of a youth justice disposal in 2008. Only three of those children committed a crime serious enough to be locked up.

The vast majority, 5,007, were given a reprimand or final warning.

Just 661 children were convicted and sentenced in the courts for crimes not serious enough to warrant custody. Of those, almost half were sentenced for the less serious summary offences. Only 41 were sentenced for more serious violence against the person offences, which include a broad range of crimes of varying severity.

But despite these children committing low-level crimes, once they enter the criminal justice system re-offending

rates for these sentences are high – 40 per cent of those given a referral order offend within a year and seven out of ten of those given a community sentence.

⇨ Three were given a custodial sentence;

⇨ 5,007 were given a reprimand or final warning;

⇨ 426 children were given a referral order, which is a community-based, restorative intervention for children who appear in court for the first time and plead guilty to an offence;

⇨ 134 were given a community sentence;

⇨ 52 were given an absolute discharge;

⇨ 24 were given a conditional discharge;

⇨ 13 were fined;

⇨ 12 were otherwise dealt with.

Total number of offences

There were 6,059 proven offences committed by children aged ten and 11 in 2008/09 – only 2.5 per cent of all offences committed by under-18-year-olds.

Data published by the Youth Justice Board shows that more than half of offences were criminal damage or theft and handling, including shoplifting. Only a quarter were

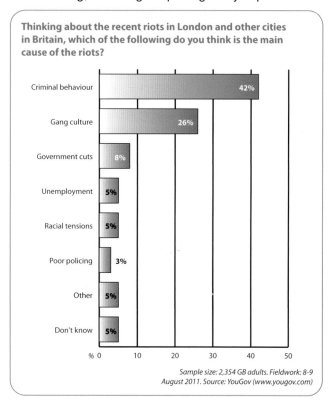

Thinking about the recent riots in London and other cities in Britain, which of the following do you think is the main cause of the riots?

Criminal behaviour	42%
Gang culture	26%
Government cuts	8%
Unemployment	5%
Racial tensions	5%
Poor policing	3%
Other	5%
Don't know	5%

Sample size: 2,354 GB adults. Fieldwork: 8-9 August 2011. Source: YouGov (www.yougov.com)

offences that are classified very broadly as violence against the person. But this includes minor assaults, which could be no more than childhood fights. The fact that relatively few of all the offences committed result in a court disposal reflects that, overall, children aged ten and 11 are involved in minor crimes.

The characteristics of children in the criminal justice system

A youth offending team manager who has many years experience working with children who offend, said:

'The ten- and 11-year-olds on our caseloads have very high welfare needs. Many have speech and learning difficulties and operate at a level well below their age. They come from extremely chaotic family backgrounds and are often on the cusp of going into care. The youth justice system is not geared up to meet the needs of these young children.'

Research does not tend to break down the characteristics of children based on age so it is not possible to identify those characteristics specific to children under the age of 12; however, we do know that children in the criminal justice system are predominantly drawn from the poorest and most disadvantaged families and communities and have multiple problems:

⇨ 60 per cent have significant speech, language or communication difficulties.

⇨ 24 to 30 per cent have a learning disability.

⇨ 18 per cent suffer from depression.

⇨ 10 per cent have anxiety disorders.

⇨ Five per cent have psychotic-like symptoms.

Why raise the age?

Criminalising children as young as ten and 11 for less serious crimes is an ineffective means of punishment. Subjecting children to criminal interventions at such a young age means they may be more likely to commit further offences and continue on the conveyor belt of crime.

Re-offending rates for children given a criminal justice disposal are high

45 per cent for those receiving a first tier penalty such as a fine, discharge or referral order, 68 per cent for those given a community order and 74 per cent for those sentenced to custody. This suggests that these interventions fail to instil a sense of personal responsibility. In contrast, multi-professional family support teams that a number of local authorities have established, such as Southend and Westminster, have demonstrated that key worker-led whole family interventions can more effectively reduce offending and anti-social behaviour by children.

Youth justice disposals are ineffective at tackling the causes of offending and do not ensure services intervene early and robustly

Individual youth justice disposals are very poor at addressing the multiple factors most closely associated with youth crime amongst ten- and 11-year-olds – social disadvantage, emotional and behavioural difficulties, poor parenting and difficulties at school. Of particular concern is that current disposals deal primarily with the child and, critically, fail to view his or her poor behaviour in the context of the whole family. Because they fail to take a systemic, whole-family approach they are not tough on the causes of crime but are very weak on them. In particular, youth justice sanctions fail to effectively respond to children's behaviour at the critical transition point from primary to secondary school.

Early criminalisation has harmful consequences

There is a strong body of research evidence demonstrating that if children are criminalised from a young age they are more likely to be drawn further and deeper into the criminal justice system, ultimately resulting in a period in custody. This is reflected in the analysis of the case files in our report *Locking Up or Giving Up?* which found that a third of children under 15 in custody were ten or 11 when first convicted. Detailed longitudinal research, involving a cohort of 4,100 children in Scotland, concluded that the deeper that children penetrate the youth justice system, the more 'damaged' they are likely to become and the less likely they are to stop offending and grow out of crime.

Avoiding criminalisation is a means of real cost avoidance

Effective intervention to tackle the multiplicity of problems that a child and his or her family is facing can substantially reduce costs to the state. Almost £6 million could have been saved in court appearances alone, of which there were 664 in 2008, money which would have been better invested in prevention rather than punishment.

Looking at James' life with the benefit of hindsight, we can see that he might well have gained a lot from early parenting support, anger management, learning support and mentoring. If these had been provided early on when he was first cautioned by the police, and continued throughout James' teenage years, instead of resorting to criminal justice responses, some or all of his offending might have been avoided. The costs of these support services would have been £42,000 up to the time he was 16, compared with the actual costs of £154,000 for the services he did receive (which include expensive court appearances and custody), a saving of more than £110,000.

Alternatives to criminalisation and prosecution

There are a number of alternatives that are not a soft option and are a more effective response than criminalisation. They successfully challenge and support children aged ten and 11 and their parents to:

⇨ face up to their behaviour;

⇨ accept responsibility for their actions;

⇨ understand and recognise the consequences for others of their behaviour;

⇨ operate within clearly set boundaries that involve the threat of sanctions;

⇨ improve school attendance and performance;

⇨ improve relationships within their family;

⇨ improve their behaviour, therefore reducing the likelihood of offending.

C'mon son, the view's much nicer this way!

POSITIVE OUTCOMES...

Multi-professional intensive family support

A number of local authorities have set up multi-professional teams, for example, the Westminster Recovery Programme, which are delivering key worker-led, co-ordinated packages of support to families with multiple problems, including children at risk of, or those who have been involved in, criminal behaviour. Rather than the child being prosecuted and receiving a youth justice disposal, these teams take a whole family approach to change behaviour.

Family intervention projects

Barnardo's runs a number of family intervention projects (FIPs) and these challenge and support parents and their children to face up to their behaviour and accept responsibility for their actions. By adopting a key worker system that takes a whole-family approach, projects have successfully improved outcomes.

Evaluation of the FIPs shows positive outcomes including 64 per cent reduction in anti-social behaviour, 58 per cent reduction in truancy, exclusions and bad behaviour at school, 61 per cent reduction in domestic violence, 45 per cent reduction in substance misuse and 42 per cent reduction in concerns about child protection.

A mother who had parenting support from Barnardo's FIP programme in Gateshead whose 11-year-old son was involved with the youth offending team, recently wrote to Tim Loughton, Parliamentary Under-Secretary for Children's Families:

'I just used to sit and cry and the boys had to look after themselves. We had no ground rules, we were like lodgers living in the same house.

'We were taught about different ways of disciplining children, actions and consequences, how to talk to and not at them. I completed the ten-week course and my life and that of my children changed 100 per cent. We now work together on problems, we talk instead of shouting, the children know what is acceptable and the consequences of doing things they know are wrong.'

Civil court orders

Two civil court orders – Child Safety Orders and Parenting Orders – are available and can be used as an effective sanction, directed at parents and families if they fail to comply with voluntary interventions, or in addition to them. The orders could be used more widely if necessary and where families fail to co-operate on a voluntary basis.

⇨ The above information is an extract from the Barnardo's report *From playground to prison*, and is reprinted with permission. Visit www.barnardos.org.uk for more information, or to view references for this piece.

© Barnardo's 2010

BARNARDO'S

T2A alliance calls for sentencing reform

Young offenders should be tried on the basis of their maturity, poll finds.

⇨ More people think that sentencing should be based on the emotional and psychological maturity of the offender rather than on their age.

⇨ Cross-party support – 81% of MPs – for maturity being taken into account by the courts.

⇨ Majority of people think young adults mature later than the current age (18) recognised by the sentencing system.

⇨ Older generations think maturity comes later in life than younger generations.

⇨ There is more support amongst Coalition MPs for sentencing young adults on a case by case basis or as a distinct group than there is for treating them as older adults.

⇨ Coalition MPs are more progressive on sentencing than Labour.

A ComRes poll conducted on behalf of the Transition to Adulthood (T2A) Alliance has found that both the public (69%) and parliamentarians (81%) believe emotional and psychological maturity should be taken into account when sentencing young adults. Currently an individual is sentenced on the basis of their age, with under-18s subject to the youth system and over-18s subject to the law as it applies to adults.

The poll supports the T2A Alliance's argument that, as people mature at different rates and many young adults in trouble with the law exhibit developmental levels characteristic of far younger people, courts should treat 18- to 24-year-olds on a case by case basis according to their maturity. This currently happens in Germany, where young adult offenders can be dealt with either in the adult or juvenile system depending on psychological and emotional assessments of their maturity.

Politically, the poll should embolden Coalition figures who have been leading criminal justice reforms in the direction the T2A Alliance recommends. A large majority of Coalition MPs (74%) think that maturity should be taken into account when sentencing a young person. Coalition MPs are also more likely to think that young adults should be sentenced either on a case by case basis or as a distinct group, rather than treated the same as older adults. Labour differs on this issue, with a slim majority (54%) in favour of always treating young adults the same as those 25 years of age or older.

Rob Allen, Chair of the T2A Alliance said: 'This poll reveals that our criminal justice system is behind the times. Both the public and parliamentarians support our calls for a common-sense approach which doesn't assume everyone reaches full maturity on their 18th birthday.

'The fact that support services targeted at youths in the criminal justice system disappear overnight when a young person hits 18 is very damaging and it is no wonder that so many of them fall back into crime. 18- to 24-year-olds are responsible for the majority of convictions in this country. Other countries, like Germany, have long demonstrated a more constructive approach to this age group and it is reflected in their lower crime rates.

'The Government is already making some of the right noises about bridging the gap between youth and adult services but now they need to follow through and drastically improve transition measures. This poll shows such reforms would win strong public support. They would also bring down crime rates and make financial savings in the long term. There really isn't any time to waste.'

About the Transition to Adulthood (T2A) Alliance

The Transition to Adulthood (T2A) Alliance is a broad coalition of organisations and individuals working to improve the opportunities and life chances of young people in their transition to adulthood, who are at risk of committing crime and falling into the criminal justice system. The Alliance is convened by the Barrow Cadbury Trust.

About the poll

⇨ 69% of people think a person's emotional and psychological maturity should be taken into account when they are accused of breaking the law, with only 57% thinking age should be taken into account. Four in ten (41%) think age is not important compared to less than a third (28%) who believe emotional and psychological maturity is not important.

⇨ Half the public (50%) think a person reaches full intellectual maturity after the age of 22, compared to 32% who think 18-21 marks the age a person reaches full intellectual maturity.

⇨ 57% of the public think a person reaches full emotional maturity after the age of 22 – at least four years after the current age recognised by the system – compared to 27% who think 18-21 marks the age a person reaches full emotional maturity.

⇨ 18- to 24-year-olds are more likely (30%) to think a person reaches full emotional maturity at age 18-21 whereas 55- to 64-year-olds are more likely (36%) to place the age higher, at 25-30.

⇨ More than eight in ten (81%) MPs think maturity should be taken into account by the courts.

⇨ 44% of Tories and 82% of Liberal Democrat MPs think

that the decision to sentence young adults either in the adult or juvenile system should be taken on a case by case basis or based on treating them as a separate age group. Only 40% of Labour MPs think the same.

3 March 2011

⇨ Information from ComRes: www.comres.co.uk

© ComRes

'Jail is not a deterrent' in preventing knife crime

As another teenager is stabbed to death, experts in violence amongst young men tell Channel 4 News that the authorities are taking the wrong approach in dealing with knife crime.

On Wednesday, a 15-year-old boy was stabbed to death in Camberwell, south London. His death was the latest in a string of killings across Britain this year.

In London alone, five teenagers have died from stab wounds this year, including two other 15-year-olds.

Last month, it was revealed that almost 4,000 teenagers were treated for knife injuries in English hospitals in the past five years and in 2010/11, more than 80 of them were under 14.

Figures held by the Ministry of Justice revealed that an average of five under-18s per day are found guilty of carrying knives by the courts – and in the past decade, the number of 12-year-olds convicted of 'having an article with blade or point' in a public place doubled, while the number of 11-year-olds convicted has risen fourfold.

Intervention

But Patrick Regan, CEO of XLP, a charity which helps kids escape from gangs, told Channel 4 News that the debate over jail time for knife killers was not the main issue surrounding knife crime.

'For sure, jail is not a deterrent for young people, but the jails are full, so increasing prison terms is a moot point,' he said. 'We need intervention and engagement, not just enforcement by police and the law. And we need to do that at an earlier stage than we currently are.

'63 per cent of kids whose fathers are violent criminals go on to commit violent crimes, so we know where to find them at an early stage.'

He said the Government spent five times more on sending teenagers to jail – and keeping them there – than on preventive projects.

'At £165,000 to keep a teenager in jail for a year, it's in the Government's financial best interests to invest more in prevention,' he added.

Last December, Justice Secretary Ken Clarke published a Green Paper in which he proposed scrapping minimum tariffs for knife killers.

And in February, the Home Secretary Theresa May promised more than £18 million to tackle crimes involving knives, guns and gangs over the next two years.

The funding announcement came after Brooke Kinsella, whose 16-year-old brother Ben was stabbed to death in 2008, advised the Home Office on the best ways to tackle the issue.

The financial boost will be distributed among a host of anti-knife and gun charities, but will be spread thinly because of the nature of dealing with youths and gang members – turning young people's lives around must be done on a case-by-case basis.

Marek Palasinski from Lancaster University, who recently published the report *Tackling knife violence: young men view things differently* (published in the *BMJ*), said that young men who carry knives do so because they view it as a necessary response to potential threats and to the lack of protection provided by authorities.

Mr Palasinski said that although attempts to tackle knife crime are working in general, his findings suggest other factors that require attention in order to prevent injury.

He said that preventing knife injuries 'must involve promoting recognition of the low controllability and unpredictability of knives, demonstrating to young men that knives actually increase, rather than decrease, personal risk'.

His study also found that young men who do not carry knives were viewed as irresponsible and thus deserving of any violence they experience.

Mr Palasinski added that young men he studied considered the consequences of being convicted of knife-related violence – a short time in prison – as relatively trivial.

'It is almost seen as something of a badge of honour without giving away too much of their lives,' he said.

He concluded that this would suggest that longer imprisonments for knife-related convictions is as important as increased policing of knife-carrying.

The teenagers that XLP works with have created a website to increase awareness about gangs and to offer advice to those currently in gangs but too scared to leave. Go to www.fightingchance.me

12 May 2011

⇨ Information from Channel 4 News. Visit www. channel4.com for more information.

© Channel 4 News

Are we ready for gangbos?

Police and local councils gained new powers yesterday [31 January 2011] to deal with gang-related violence and crime.

By Alasdair Henderson

The new 'gang injunctions', or 'gangbos', which can be sought in the county courts against adults suspected of gang involvement, function in a similar way to ASBOs (anti-social behaviour orders), although they aim to target people involved in shootings, knife crime and other serious violence rather than low-level anti-social behaviour. But will they be a helpful measure to curb gang violence, or an unnecessary restriction on liberty?

The injunctions are tailored to individuals and can involve being banned from entering certain areas, owning certain animals (such as dangerous dogs), wearing gang 'colours', or even using the Internet. But the injunctions are not all about prohibitions; they might also impose requirements to take part in activities designed to break the individual away from gang culture, such as mentoring schemes.

The new powers were brought in by the previous Government following Birmingham City Council's failed attempt to get injunctions against suspected gang members (the Court of Appeal held that they needed to apply for an ASBO instead).

Like ASBOs, the gang injunctions are civil penalties, but breaching them is a criminal offence punishable by a fine or up to two years in prison. To apply for a gang injunction the police or local council must have evidence that the person concerned has engaged in, encouraged or assisted gang-related violence, and will need to be able to prove this on the balance of probabilities at court. They will also need to convince the court that the gang injunction is necessary to prevent the person from being involved in gang-related violence or to protect the person from such violence.

> *The injunctions are tailored to individuals and can involve being banned from entering certain areas, owning certain animals (such as dangerous dogs), wearing gang 'colours', or even using the Internet*

At present the gang injunctions are available only against people aged 18 or over, but a pilot scheme allowing their use against 14- to 17-year-olds is due to start later in the year.

Another attack on civil liberties or a useful new tool?

Like ASBOs before them, gang injunction powers have immediately proved controversial. Home Office minister James Brokenshire is quoted as saying that the Government was 'not expecting huge numbers' of gang injunctions to be issued. But the same was said of ASBOs, and in fact local councils rushed to use them. The result has been that more than half of all ASBOs issued have been breached, and they have arguably proved largely ineffective.

Liberty has raised concerns that the gang injunctions will be similarly ineffective and will actually lead to negative results:

'[E]xperience with such injunctions in America suggests that they have not been effective and worse still, that they are counter-productive and have led to discrimination and stigmatisation of many innocent, minority ethnic, young people.'

Reasons for not reporting crime to the police. All BCS crime, England and Wales, 2009/10.

Reason	%
Trivial/no loss/police would not/could not do anything[1]	75%
Private/dealt with ourselves	15%
Inconvenient to report	6%
Reported to other authorities	6%
Common occurrence	2%
Fear of reprisal	2%
Dislike or fear of the police/previous bad experience with the police or courts	2%
Other[2]	6%

% 0   20   40   60   80

1. These are merged due to the similarity in their definition: for example, a respondent who thinks the incident was too trivial may code the incident as 'too trivial, no loss' or 'the police would not be interested' as these two codes may be understood as meaning the same.
2. This category includes: something that happens as part of my job; partly my/friend's/relative's fault; offender not responsible for actions; thought someone else had reported incident; similar incidents; tried to report but was not able to contact the police/police not interested; other.

Source: table 2.12, Crime in England and Wales 2009/10 (Home Office statistical bulletin). Crown copyright.

UK HUMAN RIGHTS BLOG

As with ASBOs, groups such as Liberty have also expressed reservations about the blurring of the civil and criminal law. An application for a gang injunction is dealt with on evidence of broader suspicion of involvement with gangs, rather than a specific offence, and the civil standard of proof applies. Yet a person who is under a gang injunction may face criminal penalties, including a prison sentence, if he or she breaches it.

This is a particular problem if the injunctions are applied to children. Although it seems at first preferable to deal with teenage gang members through the civil justice system, and use gang injunctions to protect them from gangs and attempt to break any ties with them, there is a danger that in fact young people will end up being pushed into the criminal justice system (through breach of an injunction) even if they have not been convicted of any specific crime.

The injunctions potentially involve quite serious infringements on people's rights to liberty, private life and free association and assembly. Articles 8 and 11 are qualified rights, and can be infringed or restricted in a fairly wide range of circumstances. For example, the police have wide-ranging general powers to deal with public assemblies of any kind in the Public Order Act 1986. However, in order to be justified, restrictions of the right must be carefully considered.

The Government's position is that although the use of gang injunctions might infringe the rights of the individual subject to the injunction, the rights of the broader community are enhanced. But this is arguably far too broad an attempted justification for such a sweeping set of new powers (reminiscent of the justification for control orders, many examples of which have of course been struck down by the courts). Liberty attacks this position, arguing that:

'While many rights are limited and are required to be balanced against the rights of others, this does not give a green light for imposing manifestly unfair proposals with such clumsy justifications. Followed to its logical conclusion, this type of oversimplification would allow any type of policy if the Government perceives that there is a benefit to be had.'

This may be overly critical. Gangs are a blight on many of Britain's towns and cities, and in many individual cases the gang injunctions may be useful tools and a justifiable restriction on gang members' rights. Several youth workers and mentors have expressed cautious support for the new powers.

But to be effective and justifiable the injunctions must be used carefully and sparingly. If the experience of ASBOs is anything to go by, that will not be the case in practice. There is a real danger, therefore, that gang injunctions may be another example of the Coalition undermining civil liberties, despite its aim to restore them. It might be better to focus more on prosecuting gang members and gang violence, rather than looking to new powers as a cure-all.

1 February 2011

⇨ The above information is reprinted with kind permission from the UK Human Rights Blog. Visit http://ukhumanrightsblog.com for more information on this and other related topics.

© UK Human Rights Blog

Our dedication to the death penalty

Half a century on from its abolition, why is capital punishment still so popular?

By Francis Welch

Almost 50 years ago a Labour MP, Sidney Silverman, proposed a Bill that would cease all state executions in Britain. The last death sentences were carried out on Peter Anthony Allen and Gwynne Owen Evans on 13 August 1964. But before Silverman's historic Bill – and ever since – a majority of the British public has consistently supported capital punishment. A YouGov survey in 2010 showed that 51% would back the reintroduction of the death penalty, with only 37% committed to its abolition.

The abolition of the death penalty was part of a wider series of liberal reforms passed in Parliament with cross-party support from the late 1960s onwards. The legalisation of abortion and decriminalisation of homosexuality in 1967 helped shape modern Britain. Harold Wilson's Government would set the standard for equality with the Equal Pay Act (1970), the Sex Discrimination Act (1975) and the Race Relations Act (1976). But whereas most people support these initiatives, the argument about whether the state should be able to execute its citizens still divides us. Less than a year after Silverman's Bill was passed, Ian Brady and Myra Hindley were arrested for the Moors murders and public opinion favoured their execution.

So why, after half a century without state executions, are most people not convinced? One reason could be the public's expectation that the law should act on their behalf. The *Telegraph*'s Simon Heffer told me for the *Crime and Punishment – The Story of Capital Punishment* documentary that, for the most serious homicides, in the 'interest of maintaining confidence in the rule of law the only appropriate punishment is the death penalty'.

He cites the cases of murderers convicted of the most heinous crimes, where torture, rape and ultimately murder were premeditated against children or the very old. The public would appear to back this view. When Ian Huntley was arrested for the murders of Jessica Chapman and Holly Wells, a YouGov poll showed that 63% of respondents believed Huntley should be executed by the state. The tabloid press also stirs up public frustration with stories of re-offending sex attackers and murderers enjoying a comfortable prison term. And while the tabloids don't support the reintroduction of the death penalty in their editorial pages, they do allow their high-profile columnists to call for the return of the noose.

Professor Robert Blecker from the New York Law School believes that citizens have the right to expect that the state will deliver retribution on their behalf – and indeed that the state has an obligation to do so. Blecker cites Kant to argue that even a civilised state has 'a moral imperative and a duty' to act and that if you break society's rules by committing murder then as 'a responsible agent, you've chosen to do what you did, then you deserve to die for it'.

> *A YouGov survey in 2010 showed that 51% would back the reintroduction of the death penalty, with only 37% committed to its abolition*

Opponents to capital punishment, like Geoffrey Robertson QC, argue that it is 'much worse for an individual to spend the rest of their life in prison than to be executed immediately'. But most of the public don't share his faith in the prison system. It was the Victorians who first introduced the idea of imprisonment as an alternative to execution. This was part of a liberal reforming agenda, which sought a more proportional sense of punishment. As a consequence, conviction rates rose as juries became more likely to convict. The penal system has been used since to maintain the public's faith in the law. After abolition those convicted of murder received a mandatory life sentence and in 1983 the whole life tariff was introduced, meaning some prisoners would never be released. But while convicted murderers spend considerably longer in prison today than they did before the death penalty was abolished, it's questionable whether in cases like the Soham murders the public are convinced that prison is a satisfactory alternative.

But what about miscarriages of justice, like the case of Derek Bentley, who was posthumously pardoned four decades after being hung? Michael Mansfield QC believes that the ultimate sanction 'can't be applied in a flawed system of justice'. Mansfield represented both the Birmingham Six and Guildford Four, all of whom would almost certainly have been executed had Britain retained capital punishment. The former Home Secretary Michael Howard admits these cases changed his mind on the death penalty. 'I accepted that you could never completely eliminate the chance of a mistake and since then I have been averse to the idea of the state deliberately taking someone's life.'

THE GUARDIAN

During the 1980s and early 1990s a free vote was held every year in Parliament on the reintroduction of capital punishment. One MP who always voted in favour of a return of the death penalty was Ann Widdecombe, a former prisons minister, who argues that 'during the height of the IRA outrages, there was a strong moral case for saying a moral deterrent is available' and that only the death penalty could provide this.

This defence has been put forward since the era of the Bloody Code in the 18th century, when over 200 offences – including stealing a rabbit or keeping the company of gypsies – carried the death sentence. Until 1868 executions were carried out in public in front of drunken and baying crowds and it was expected that the public would attend to witness justice being carried out. Professor Vic Gatrell of Cambridge University, author of *The Hanging Tree: Execution and the English People*, explains that this public spectacle was designed as a visual show of the state's power and to 'testify to the anger of the king'. But this was before the Victorians established a penal system and a police force. And after decades of research the contention that the death penalty is a deterrent in countries that still enforce it, like the US and China, has not been proved either way.

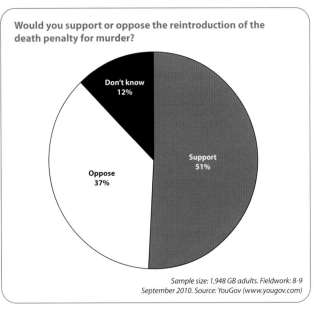

Would you support or oppose the reintroduction of the death penalty for murder?

Don't know 12%

Support 51%

Oppose 37%

Sample size: 1,948 GB adults. Fieldwork: 8-9 September 2010. Source: YouGov (www.yougov.com)

Capital punishment was only fully removed from British statutes under the Crime and Disorder Act 1998: until this time it had been technically possible to be executed by the state for treason or piracy. As long as Britain remains committed to its human rights legislation, it will never reintroduce capital punishment, and all the major political parties oppose it. Abolition was led by MPs who considered it a moral issue and would not be swayed by public opinion. But with the public still largely unconvinced, one wonders whether they would maintain their opposition now.

5 April 2011

Death penalty in the US

Facts and statistics about capital punishment in the United States.

In September 2011, after ten years on death row, inmate Troy Davis was executed in the US state of Georgia. After the majority of witnesses in the case retracted their original statements, Davis' sentence sparked a torrent of media coverage and international protests. At the same time, in Texas, white supremacist Lawrence Brewer was executed for the racially-motivated murder of James Byrd Jr. These two very different cases illustrate the debate surrounding the death penalty in the US. Here are just some of the facts and figures:

⇨ In the US, the death penalty is used as punishment for capital offences such as first-degree murder.

⇨ Of the 50 US states, 35 use the death penalty. New Mexico abolished the death penalty in 2009, but the act was not retroactive, leaving two prisoners awaiting execution.

⇨ Since 1973, over 130 people have been released from death row with evidence of their innocence.

⇨ California, Florida, and Texas hold the most death row inmates.

⇨ Of the 35 states currently using the death penalty, Texas executes the highest percentage of inmates per year. There have been 463 executions in Texas since 1976.

⇨ In January 2010 there were 61 women on death row, 1.9% of the total death row population.

⇨ The majority of states use lethal injection as their primary method of execution,. Other methods include electrocution, gassing and hanging.

⇨ It is estimated that enforcing the death penalty in Florida costs the state $51 million a year more than it would cost to sentence all first-degree murderers to life in prison without parole.

⇨ 96% of states that have reviewed the relationship between race and the death penalty have concluded a pattern of either race-of-victim or race-of-defendant discrimination, or both.

⇨ There have been a total of 1,226 executions in the US since 1976.

Facts taken from the Facts about the Death Penalty *report by the Death Penalty Information Center, Washington, US, September 2010.*

As Britain debates the death penalty again, studies from America confirm that it works

By Tim Stanley

Britain is talking seriously about the death penalty for the first time in over a decade. It was last discussed in Parliament when the Human Rights Act was passed in 1998, and now blogger Paul Staines (of Guido Fawkes fame) is petitioning for another House of Commons debate in 2011. We can expect anti-death penalty campaigners to point to America as an example of why it should stay banned. The usual images will be invoked of pot-bellied, racist, white judges sentencing innocent saints to death by chainsaw in some Alabama charnel house. Accepting the many obvious injustices in the US legal system, there is an instinctive British snobbery towards Americans that renders any comparison between our two countries unflattering. Amnesty International, Liberty and the New Statesman will probably ask, 'Why would we endorse a system of retribution practised by those knuckle-dragging, Bible bashing, toothless crazies over in Texas?' Well, here's one good reason: it works.

From 2001 to 2007, 12 academic studies were carried out in the US that examined the impact of the death penalty on local crime rates. They explored the hypothesis that as the potential cost of an action increases, so people are deterred from doing it. Nine out of 12 of the studies concluded that the death penalty saves lives. Some of their findings are stunning. Professors at Emory University determined that each execution deters an average of 18 murders. Another Emory study found that speeding up executions strengthens deterrence: for every 2.75 years cut from an inmate's stay on death row, one murder would be prevented. Illinois has just voted to stop executions across the state. According to a University of Houston study, that could be a fatal mistake. It discovered that an earlier Illinois moratorium in 2000 encouraged 150 additional homicides in four years.

Opponents will point out that the death penalty is practised in the states with the highest murder rates. This is true, but it doesn't mean that executions don't work – it just means that they take place where they are needed most. The states without the death penalty historically have lower than average levels of crime. When the death penalty was suspended nationwide from 1968 to 1976, murder rates went through the roof – except in those states. When the ban was lifted, the states that reintroduced the death penalty saw an astonishing 38 per cent fall in their murder rate over 20 years. Indeed, there is a statistical relationship between the growth in executions and the decline in murder.

According to John Lott, author of *Freedomnomics*, 'between 1991 and 2000, there were 9,114 fewer murders per year, while the number of executions per year rose by 71'. In his own studies, the only exception to this rule proved to be multiple victim public shootings, like the Virginia Tech Massacre. The reason is obvious: the perpetrators expect to die while carrying out their crime and invariably do.

> **Britain is talking seriously about the death penalty for the first time in over a decade. It was last discussed in Parliament when the Human Rights Act was passed in 1998**

There are many failings in the US justice system; the use of the death penalty can be symptomatic of them, but it is not a cause. For example, it is incredibly costly to execute a criminal. According to one anti-death penalty group, 'The California death penalty system costs taxpayers $114 million per year beyond the costs of keeping convicts locked up for life. Taxpayers have paid more than $250 million for each of the state's executions.' But the reason for the decades criminals spend waiting for their execution is simple: money-hungry lawyers and sympathetic liberals keep on appealing their sentences. Another complaint is that the death penalty is biased toward black defendants. Tragically, this is true: 42 per cent of death row inmates are black. However, this reflects appalling indices of poverty, social dysfunction and racism. It is not necessarily a comment upon the appropriateness of the sentence. Many states have taken the decision that, on balance, justice should not be suspended altogether just because it is applied unevenly. That's tough and needs addressing, but law and order trumps abstract notions of equality in the minds of most voters.

But for anyone who wallows in the superiority of the UK justice system, with its human rights legislation and touchy-feely approach to child murderers, it is worth bearing in mind that our rate of violent crime is actually far higher than that of the United States. According to a 2009 study, there were 2,034 offences per 100,000 people that year in the UK, putting Britain at the top of the international league table. America recorded just 466. The US seems to be getting something right: executing cold-blooded killers might be part of it.

5 August 2011

THE TELEGRAPH

⇨ The latest crime and justice survey estimated 874,000 crimes were committed in 2010/11, including 220,000 violent crimes. (page 2)

⇨ There is a clear pattern from the British Crime Survey (BCS) of crime reaching a peak in 1995 with a subsequent decline, with overall BCS crime down by 50 per cent since 1995. (page 3)

⇨ Police-recorded violence against the person fell by four per cent between 2008/09 and 2009/10. Longer-term trends from the BCS show violent crime down by 50 per cent from its peak in 1995. (page 4)

⇨ There were 54,509 sexual offences recorded by the police in 2009/10, a six per cent increase compared with 2008/09. (page 5)

⇨ 50% of young people surveyed think the cause of the riots was mindless violence: the rest say boredom (13.5%), lack of provision/interest in young (13.2%), lack of morals (10.6%), gap between rich and poor (6.6%) and youth unemployment (6%). (page 10)

⇨ A research study which followed 1,800 people from age three to 23 found that individuals with poor amygdala function in early life were more likely to become criminal offenders later on. (page 11)

⇨ The vast majority of young people are not involved in violence or gangs and want nothing to do with them. (page 13)

⇨ If you get a 'suspended' prison sentence you don't go to prison immediately, but serve your sentence in the community. If you break any conditions, or commit another crime, you will go to prison to serve your sentence. (page 19)

⇨ New plans for community sentences propose four days of hard manual labour, improving public areas by clearing up litter, cleaning graffiti and maintaining parks and other green spaces. The fifth day will be spent looking for full-time employment. (page 20)

⇨ Justice Secretary Ken Clarke has announced a new sentencing regime that will see more mandatory life sentences for a broader range of crimes. (page 21)

⇨ A new FBI-style crime-fighting agency will target drug gangs and paedophiles as well as helping to police Britain's borders, the Home Secretary has said. (page 22)

⇨ Over 17% of the UK population between the ages of 18 and 52 have a criminal conviction. (page 26)

⇨ Reoffending rates are greatly influenced by whether a person finds work or not. Employment is often quoted as the most important factor in helping to reduce reoffending rates. (page 26)

⇨ The criminal justice system in England and Wales does very little to foster communication between the offender and the offended, with restorative justice programmes being made available in less than 1% of cases. (page 29)

⇨ The minimum age of criminal responsibility in England and Wales was set at ten in the 1963 Children and Young Person's Act. Previously the 1908 Children Act set it at seven. (page 30)

⇨ More people think that sentencing should be based on the emotional and psychological maturity of the offender rather than on their age. (page 33)

⇨ More than eight in ten (81%) MPs think maturity should be taken into account by the courts. (page 33)

⇨ Figures held by the Ministry of Justice revealed that an average of five under-18s per day are found guilty of carrying knives by the courts – and in the past decade, the number of 12-year-olds convicted of 'having an article with blade or point' in a public place doubled, while the number of 11-year-olds convicted has risen fourfold. (page 34)

⇨ There have been a total of 1,226 executions in the US since 1976. (page 38)

2011 England riots

Between 6 and 10 August 2011, widespread rioting and looting broke out in London, Manchester and other cities across England following a peaceful march to protest the shooting of a young Londoner, Mark Duggan, by police. Five people died and at least 16 were injured as a result of the riots. The riots have given rise to significant debate surrounding gang culture and youth crime, the causes of social breakdown and the effectiveness of police action in dealing with the problem.

Age of criminal responsibility

The minimum age of criminal responsibility in England and Wales was set at ten in the 1963 Children and Young Person's Act. In the 1998 Crime and Disorder Act, Labour abolished the principle of *doli incapax*, whereby the prosecution had to prove that a child under 14 appearing in the criminal court knew and fully understood what he or she was doing was seriously wrong.

In Scotland, while the age of responsibility is eight years, a child below the age of twelve cannot be prosecuted.

Crime

Crime may be defined as an act or omission prohibited or punished by law. A 'criminal offence' includes any infringement of the criminal law, from homicide to riding a bicycle without lights. What is classified as a crime is supposed to reflect the values of society and to reinforce those values. If an act is regarded as harmful to society or its citizens, it is often, but not always, classified as a criminal offence.

Custody

In criminal terminology, being 'in custody' refers to someone being held in spite of their wishes, either by the police while awaiting trial (remanded in custody), or, having received a custodial sentence, in prison or other secure accommodation. If someone has spent time on remand, that time is taken off their prison sentence.

Deterrent

Any threat or punishment which is seen to deter someone from a certain action: the threat of prison, for example, is expected to function as a deterrent to criminal behaviour.

'Gangbo'

'Gang injunctions' or 'gangbos' are new powers which can be sought against adults suspected of gang involvement. They function in a similar way to ASBOs (anti-social behaviour orders), although they aim to target people involved in shootings, knife crime and other serious violence rather than low-level anti-social behaviour. They are tailored to individuals and can involve being banned from entering certain areas, owning certain animals or even using the Internet.

Non-custodial sentence

A punishment which does not require someone convicted of a crime to be held in prison or another closed institution. Community sentences, restraining orders and fines are all types of non-custodial punishment.

Rehabilitation

The process by which an offender can learn, through therapy and education, to be a useful member of society on completing their sentence.

Reoffending rate

The rate at which offenders, having been convicted of a crime and punished, will then go on to commit another crime (implying that the punishment was ineffectual as a crime deterrent).

Restorative justice

This usually involves communication between an offender and their victim, family members, and possibly other people from the community or people affected by the crime. The purpose of the communication is to discuss the offending behaviour and come up with ways for the person to 'repay' the victim or community for their crime.

Sentence

The punishment given by a judge to a convicted offender at the end of a criminal trial. This generally takes the form of a fine, a community punishment, a discharge or a period of imprisonment.

ACKNOWLEDGEMENTS

The publisher is grateful for permission to reproduce the following material.

While every care has been taken to trace and acknowledge copyright, the publisher tenders its apology for any accidental infringement or where copyright has proved untraceable. The publisher would be pleased to come to a suitable arrangement in any such case with the rightful owner.

Chapter One: Crime Trends

Crime on your street revealed, © Crown copyright is reproduced with the permission of Her Majesty's Stationery Office, Crime 'affecting fewer people', © 2011 The Press Association. All rights reserved, Crime in England and Wales 2009/10, © Crown copyright is reproduced with the permission of Her Majesty's Stationery Office, Troublesome youth groups, gangs and knife-carrying in Scotland, © Crown copyright is reproduced with the permission of Her Majesty's Stationery Office, Riots and rationality, © Economic and Social Research Council, Young people must be consulted on the causes of violence, © Children & Young People Now, Over 500 young people tell the Jack Petchey Foundation what they think about the rioting, © Jack Petchey Foundation, Are criminals programmed to offend?, © Criminologist.

Chapter Two: Crime Prevention

Reporting a crime, © Crown copyright is reproduced with the permission of Her Majesty's Stationery Office, Ending gang and youth violence, © Crown copyright is reproduced with the permission of Her Majesty's Stationery Office, Schools at the sharp end of knife crime education, © Guardian News and Media Limited 2011, Why ex-offenders should be given a role in cutting youth crime, © Guardian News and Media Limited 2011.

Chapter Three: Criminal Justice

Types of prison sentence, © Crown copyright is reproduced with the permission of Her Majesty's Stationery Office, Changes to community sentences, © Centre for Economic and Social Inclusion, New sentences to 'restore clarity and common sense', © info4security, FBI-style crime agency to lead fight against drug gangs, © Channel 4 News, Breaking the cycle, © Clinks, Prejudged: tagged for life, © Working Links, Restorative justice after the riots?, © Guardian News and Media Limited 2011, Children 'not facing harsh riot sentences', © Children & Young People Now, From playground to prison, © Barnardo's 2010, T2A alliance calls for sentencing reform, © ComRes, 'Jail is not a deterrent' in preventing knife crime, © Channel 4 News, Are we ready for gangbos?, © UK Human Rights Blog, Our dedication to the death penalty, © Guardian News and Media Limited 2011, Death penalty in the US, © Independence Educational Publishers, As Britain debates the death penalty again, studies from America confirm that it works, © Telegraph Media Group Limited 2011.

Illustrations

Pages 1, 19, 27, 32: Don Hatcher; pages 7, 10: Bev Aisbett; pages 8, 18, 28, 36: Simon Kneebone; pages 9, 15, 24: Angelo Madrid.

Cover photography

Left: © Jason Conlon. Centre: © Michal Zacharzewski. Right: © Shad Gross.

Additional acknowledgements

With thanks to the Independence team: Mary Chapman, Sandra Dennis and Jan Sunderland.

Lisa Firth
Cambridge
January, 2012

ASSIGNMENTS

The following tasks aim to help you think through the debate surrounding crime and punishment and provide a better understanding of the topic.

1 'The 2011 riots were caused by a feral underclass of young people who believe the law does not apply to them. There is never any excuse for criminal behaviour.' Do you agree with this opinion? Discuss your views in small groups, playing 'devil's advocate' where necessary to stimulate a lively debate.

2 Read *Crime 'affecting fewer people'* on page 2 and have a look at the figures on pages 3-5. Why do you think there is a common perception among some people that crime is rising, even though Government statistics appear to show that in most categories it is falling?

3 Read *Troublesome youth groups, gangs and knife-carrying in Scotland* on pages 6-7. How do you think young people become involved in gang culture, some from a very early age? Design a poster which could be displayed in schools, encouraging young people to resist the lure of gangs and violent crime.

4 Do you think films such as 'Ocean's 11' or 'Lock, Stock and Two Smoking Barrels' glamourise crime and criminal activity? What about video games such as the 'Grand Theft Auto' series? Give reasons for your answer.

5 What is the primary purpose of prison: retribution or rehabilitation? Do you think conditions in prison are too severe/not severe enough? Do they offer enough opportunities for education and therapy which might help a criminal leave his or her old life behind?

6 Read *Restorative justice after the riots* on pages 28-29. Write a letter from a shopkeeper whose small business was looted and vandalised, to the rioters who caused the damage. Explain how their actions affected you, both in practical terms (i.e. the amount of money lost) and emotionally. How do you think the rioters might feel on reading the letter from their victim?

7 Write a short story about someone drawn into a criminal lifestyle, and their attempt to rebuild their life following a spell in prison.

8 'This house believes that a ten-year-old does not have the emotional maturity to be held responsible for their actions. The age of criminal responsibility should be raised to 14.' Debate this motion as a class, with one half arguing in favour and the other against. Read *From playground to prison* on pages 30-32 for some background information.

9 'When young children commit crimes, it must be because of a lack of discipline and moral education at home. Their parents should be punished for the crime the child has committed, since it has been caused by their neglect.' Is this a fair opinion? Write a brief article, weighing up the arguments for and against this view and giving your own opinion.

10 Read *Prejudged: tagged for life* on pages 26-27. If you were an employer, would you consider employing an ex-offender? What might your concerns be? What might be the concerns of the ex-offender? In pairs, role play a job interview between a rehabilitated ex-offender and an employer.

11 'Some crimes are so horrific, the death penalty is the only appropriate punishment. The victim's loved ones deserve that.' 'The main problem with the death penalty is we can never be 100% sure of someone's guilt. That is why it should never be reintroduced.' Do you agree with either of these views? What other arguments might be put forward for and against the death penalty? Write a summary of the arguments for and against, and give your own conclusion.

12 Winnie Johnson, whose 12-year-old son Keith Bennett was killed by the 'moors murderers' Ian Brady and Myra Hindley in 1964, has been quoted as saying that she does not support the reintroduction of the death penalty as 'hanging is too quick'. Do you agree with this view? Should more weight be given to victims' relatives and friends when it comes to deciding the appropriate punishment for offenders?

13 Watch the 1991 British film 'Let Him Have It' starring Christopher Eccleston, which is based on a true story. and write a review. In what way can cases such as that of Derek Bentley inform the debate surrounding capital punishment?